SOPRINTENDENZA ARCHEOLOGICA DI ROMA

DOMVS AVREA

Elisabetta Segala
Ida Sciortino

ELECTA

Texts
Elisabetta Segala (pp. 5-53)
Ida Sciortino (pp. 55-99)

Translation
Colin Swift

Reprint 2003
First Edition 1999

www.electaweb.it

SOMMARIO

NERO'S ROYAL PALACE

In July AD 64, a fire, "who knows if it was by chance or through the wickedness of the prince—the sources tell us of both versions—but certainly more serious and more terrible than any other that has struck Rome in terms of the violence of the flames" (Tacitus, *Annals*, XV, 38), raged for nine consecutive days and devastated the centre of the city, altering its appearance. The fire, according to Tacitus, began in the Circus Maximus, then spread to the low ground and from there to the hills and through the narrow, tortuous alleys of the most ancient areas. Of the fourteen regions into which the city was divided, three were completely destroyed and seven seriously damaged.

"Nero was in Antium at the time and did not come back to Rome until the fire was approaching the palace he had built to link the gardens of Maecenas to the Palatine. However, he could not stop the fire engulfing the Palatine, his palace and everything else around" (Tacitus, *Annals*, XV, 39). While the city burned and the suspicion spread that the fire had been started by order of the emperor himself, Nero "was watching this fire from the Towers of Maecenas. Dressed up in theatrical clothes and gladdened by what he called 'the beauty of the flames', he sang of the destruction of Troy (Suetonius, *Nero*, 38). This is also confirmed by Tacitus: "The rumour went around that, while the city was burning, he had jumped up on the stage of the imperial palace and sung 'The Fall of Troy', representing in this ancient calamity the present disaster" (*Annals*, XV, 39).

The palace to which the sources refer is the first of the two imperial residences built by Nero, the name of which comes down to us from Suetonius: "he called it at the beginning *transitoria* and later, destroyed by a fire and rebuilt, *aurea*" (*Nero*, 31). The features, extension and limits of this residence are not known exactly; the term *transitoria* (temporary, connecting) tells us that the house joined the building nuclei of the Palatine with the *horti* (urban villas) of the Esquiline, the *Maecenatiani*, left in inheritance to Augustus on the death of Maecenas in AD 8 and the *Lamiani*, which became imperial property under Caligula, and perhaps within the property there were a number of public roads. A lavish nymphaeum found under the Banquet Hall of the Flavian Palace on the Palatine is attributed to the *Domus Transitoria*: inside, there stood a pavilion supported by porphyry columns which covered a central fountain. Facing this, there was a recess pierced with niches ornamented by 24 small columns of porphyry and serpentine with bases and capitals in gilded bronze; behind the recess were nine water jets fed by a

1. Francesco Bartoli (Rome, 1670-1733), plan and elevation of the "Bagni di Augusto" (Palatine, Domus Transitoria). Eton College Library

stepped water cascade. On either side of the room a number of small rooms opened out symmetrically, two of which had fountains in the background and two which are recesses. The whole complex was faced with inlaid polychrome marble both on the floors and walls. The vaults were frescoed with epic scenes and dionysiac friezes. One of these, currently preserved at the Palatine Museum, has partitioned panels divided by stucco cornices which show scenes from Homer. This complex is cut by the foundations of buildings related to the *Domus Aurea* (the Golden House).

Still on the Palatine, recent excavations allow us to clarify that the residence of Tiberius (*Domus Tiberiana*) was initially, like the house of Augustus, a complex formed of late-Republican constructions. The new palace was a single project and preserves the name of Tiberius, though it is rather to be attributed to the early years of the principate of Nero and can be associated with the *Domus Transitoria*. There remains a large rectangular base which was intended to support the platform on which the actu-

2-3. Details of the vault decoration in a room in the Domus Transitoria. Rome, Palatine Museum

al palace stood, and which is subdivided by cryptoporticoes into rectangular and square areas.

A further building came to light underneath the Temple of Venus and Rome, consisting of a domed circular hall, preceded by a tetrastyle portico and flanked by a long cryptoporticus. This building has been attributed by some to Nero's *Domus Transitoria*, but today this hypothesis is considered wrong.

The destruction of most of the city centre during the fire of AD 64 allowed the emperor to expropriate a vast area of about 80 hectares and to build a new palace "which extended from the Palatine to the Esquiline... The following details will convey its size and magnificence. A colossal statue of Nero, 120 feet in height, stood in the vestibule of the house. Its width was such as to include three mile-long porticoes and a lake which resembled the sea, surrounded by buildings made to resemble cities. All around there were villas with fields, vineyards and pastures, woods full of every type of domestic and wild animal. In other parts of the palace, structures were overlaid with gold and stud-

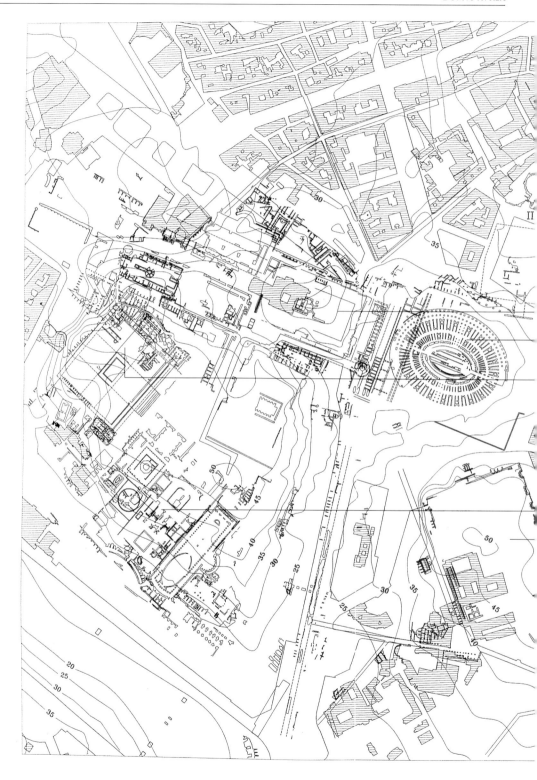

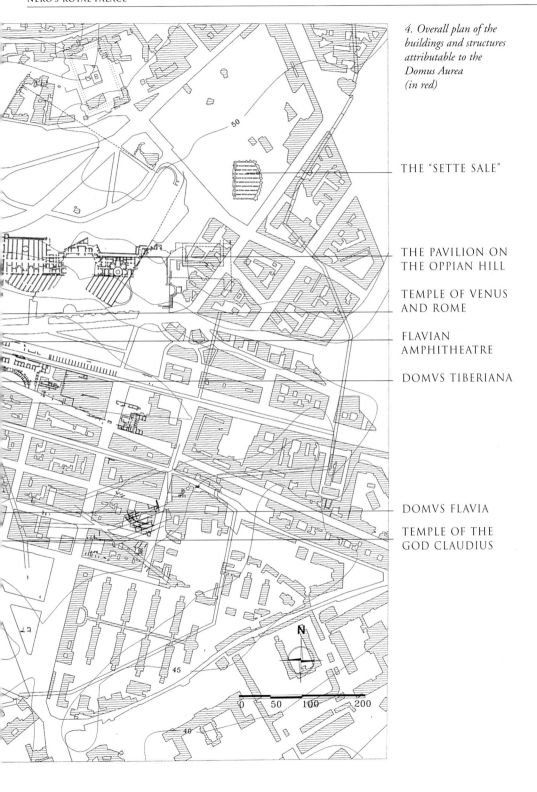

4. Overall plan of the buildings and structures attributable to the Domus Aurea (in red)

THE "SETTE SALE"

THE PAVILION ON THE OPPIAN HILL

TEMPLE OF VENUS AND ROME

FLAVIAN AMPHITHEATRE

DOMVS TIBERIANA

DOMVS FLAVIA

TEMPLE OF THE GOD CLAUDIUS

ded with gems and shells. The dining rooms had ceilings of ivory, the panels of which were mobile and perforated so that flowers and perfume could be showered upon the guests. The main dining room was circular and revolved continuously, day and night, like the earth. The baths were supplied with sea water and sulphurous water. When it was completed, Nero inaugurated the house, and he showed his satisfaction by remarking that finally he could begin to live in a house worthy of a human being" (Suetonius, *Nero*, 31).

The architects who planned and built the *Domus Aurea* were Severus and Celer, "whose fanciful daring managed to create—using art and squandering the wealth of the prince—eccentricities which went against the laws of nature" (Tacitus, *Annals*, XV, 42) The new palace of the emperor, was set out like a gigantic suburban villa in the heart of the city, and extended from the Palatine to the Velian hill, where its vestibule stood. It occupied the slopes and summit of the Oppian hill as far as the *Sette Sale*, included the imperial *horti* on the Esquiline, and arrived at the Caelian hill (having probably following the Servian walls eastwards) where it incorporated the Temple of the God Claudius, which was transformed into a monumental nymphaeum. The whole valley, at that time occupied by the artificial lake where later the Flavian Amphitheatre was to stand, was enclosed within the villa.

The novelty of conception and the vastness and lavishness of the complex amazed contemporaries but also provoked bitter criticism of the emperor. Pliny, referring to the Theatre of Pompey which Nero had overlaid with gold for the single day in which he had to show it to Tiridates the king of Armenia, stated: "and what a small thing this was compared to the *Domus Aurea,* which embraced the whole of Rome!" (*Natural History*, XXXIII, 54). And again: "twice have we seen the houses of the princes, Gaius and Nero, extend so far that they surround the city" (*Natural History*, XXXVI, 111). Martial complained (*Epigrams*, 2) that a single house occupied the whole city and famous satirical verses circulated: "Rome is now a single house: try moving to Veii, citizens, if this house does not soon occupy Veii as well!" (Suetonius, *Nero*, 39). In AD 65, at the time of the conspiracy against the emperor, Piso stated that the murder of the prince should take place in "that hated palace which Nero had plundered his people to build" (Tacitus, *Annals*, XV, 52).

This enormous complex survived for only a few years after the Nero's death in AD 68. Today it is usually only identified with the pavilion on the Oppian hill, which survived because it was incorporated within the terracing carried out for Trajan's Baths, which were built over it. However, other remains have been investigated recently which allow us to partially reconstruct the appearance of the entire *Domus Aurea.* On the Palatine, the rooms of the *Domus Transitoria* were cut by the robust foundations of a round building (perhaps with a cupola) laid after the fire of AD 64, which was contained within a water basin and which possibly could be identified as one of the dining rooms (*cenationes*) mentioned by Suetonius. Another two halls, attributable to the same building phase, have emerged under the *Aula Regia* of the Flavian Palace. Even the base of the so-called *Domus Tiberiana*

5. *The Meta Sudans, the Arch of Titus, the Temple of Venus and Rome and the Colossus in a reconstruction by Ernest-Georges Coquart (1863)*

went through a second Neronian building phase: the palace stood in the middle of the platform, surrounded by porticoes opening out on to an actual hanging garden. It was accessible by means of two stairways, one from the monumental northern façade facing the Forum and one from the eastern side. On the Velian hill, in the area currently occupied by the Temple of Venus and Rome, stood the great vestibule-atrium mentioned by Suetonius, which, as the sturdy chamber foundations discovered in the southeastern corner seem to suggest, had a number of floors. Inside the vestibule stood the work of the Greek sculptor Zenodorus, "the colossus, 119 and a half feet in height, designed to represent the emperor, dedicated to the Sun…" (Pliny, *Natural History*, XXXIV, 46). More than 35 meters high, the bronze statue was probably inspired by the Colossus of Rhodes and represented Nero with the attributes of the sun, nude, upright, the right arm held outwards leaning on a support (which in a later age took on the appearance of a rudder), the left arm bent to hold a globe. On his head he wore a crown consisting of seven rays, each six meters long. The only known representations of the Colossus, on coins of Alexander Severus and Gordianus III seem to show a Lysippian arrangement of the figure. The size of the work certainly expressed the identification of the emperor with the god: Pliny recalls that "the emperor Nero commissioned a portrait of colossal dimensions on a canvas of 120 feet, unthinkable up to that time. Once finished, this painting was struck by lightning in the Maiani gardens, and burned with the most beautiful part of the garden" (*Natural History*, XXXV, 51). The portrait matched the Colossus; it was of exactly the same height, symbolising the same absolutist conception of imperial power.

The various buildings which made up the complex of the *Domus Aurea* were the result of grandiose operations which cut and contained the hills, and the disparities in the level of the terrain had to be corrected by monumental porticoed roads. The foundations of the porticoes of one road remain; it started at an entrance propylaeum in the valley and rose towards the Palatine, skirting the vestibule. At the same time the *via Sacra*, the *clivo Palatino* and the *vicus ad Carinas* were also given porticoes. The lake (*stagnum Neronis*) was fed by the Caelimontanus aqueduct and took up a quadrangular area in the middle of the valley. It was connected scenically with the surrounding buildings, which must in fact have appeared "great, as if they were cities", by

6. Hypothetical reconstructions of the pavilion on the Oppian hill and the stagnum Neronis

means of descending terraces which opened on to an artificial inlet with porticoes, perhaps those mentioned by Suetonius. The core of the building intended to support the terraces which connected the atrium to the lake came to light in the recent excavations in the valley of the Colosseum, but similar structures have been identified at different times along the northern side of the valley. Certainly a system of terraces, containing walls, and steps must also have solved the difference in level with the Oppian hill, and linked up with the lower floor of the palace, while the upper floor of pavilions and gardens spread out on the top of the hill. Towards the south stood the base of the Temple of the God Claudius, transformed into a nymphaeum with a network of passages and fountains. If we imagine that on the opposite side the Neronian structure already envisaged the existence of baths—adapted later on by the emperor Titus—it seems obvious that the lake must have been at the heart of an extraordinary monumental arrangement. The construction of the lake erased all roads which had previously met in the valley. Only one road from east to west survived, which led from the Circus Maximus towards the Esquiline, perhaps reduced to linking-up different parts of the palace.

There was rural landscape all around, with cultivated land, woods and pasture in which both domestic and wild animals circulated. Even the old imperial *horti* on the Esquiline were incorporated into this area. The wonders of the *Domus Aurea*, according to Tacitus, "were not so much in the precious stones and gold, material whose use was by then common, trite even since wealth was the order of the day, but rather the cultivated fields and lakes with woods on one side—arising in wide deserted places and open spaces—and vast panoramas on the other" (*Annals*, XV, 42).

The practise of constructing artificial inlets, surrounding them with temporary pavilions, and populating the area with exotic birds and animals, was not new to Rome. This type of arrangement was recalled by Tacitus (*Annals,* XV, 37) in the famous banquet held by Tigellinus at the lake of Agrippa in the Campus Martius; but in the imperial palace all this was represented on a gigantic scale, not for a day, but for ever, designed to impress the onlooker with the greatness of the emperor.

As far as architecture is concerned, the *Domus Aurea* follows the example of the suburban villas of the late Republican and early imperial periods, and models itself above all on the maritime villas of Campania. These villas are characterised by a sparse distribution of buildings inserted into the landscape, which open out onto panoramic vistas over the sea, across terraces, porticoes and gardens.

The plan for the *Domus Aurea* seems to have been inspired above all by Baiae, the most luxurious and famous residential centre of the Roman world, where an imposing agglomeration of luxurious villas, bath buildings, and pleasure spots extended from the hills and around to the coast. It was indeed for Baiae that Nero had conceived two great projects: the first, again with Severus and Celer as the architects, was the construction of a navigable canal from Lake Avernus to the mouth of the Tiber, a total length of 160 miles; the second was the construction of a covered lake, surrounded by porticoes and filled with the thermal waters of Baiae, from Capo Misenum to Lake Avernus (Tacitus, *Annals,* XV, 42; Suetonius, *Nero,* 31).

Besides the economic reasons which might have encouraged Nero to attempt the first project, it is obvious that the canal would have physically linked Baiae and Rome, while at the same time reinforcing a symbolic link. It seems natural therefore that through a scenic arrangement of series of buildings on the Roman hills which, by means of porticoes and terraces, opened out on to a rural panorama and on to a view of a lake—according to Suetonius, almost a sea—Nero indeed wished to emulate the landscape of Baiae.

The novelty of the project was in its grand scale and in the fact that the complex occupied the heart of the city, but also in the ideological significance which it held. After the fire of AD 64,

7. Small picture with maritime villa from Stabiae.
Naples, Museo Archeologico Nazionale

8. Small pictures with representations of otium villae, from Pompeii.
Naples, Museo Archeologico Nazionale

Nero began to represent himself as the Sun and as the initiator of a new golden age, during which "the earth produced fruits with a fertility never seen before and there were treasures within reach offered by the gods" (Tacitus, *Annals*, XVI, 2). The residence of the emperor thus became the royal palace of the Sun, radiant with gold. This ideological interpretation seems to parallel the descriptions which have come down to us from the literary sources – according to which the whole house was covered with gold and gems – and archaeological data, which confirms a widespread use of gold-leaf on the frescoes and stuccoes. What is more, at least with regard to the pavilion on the Oppian hill, we know that an accurate analysis of the use of light must also have influenced the choice of materials. Pliny says that after the fire of AD 64 the Temple of Fortune of Sejanus, which at that time was incorporated within the *Domus Aurea*, was rebuilt with a stone called *phengites*, perhaps an alabaster from Cappadocia. "Thanks to the stone, even when the doors were shut there was a gleam inside like day, but the effect was different to that which is found with the *specularis lapis*: it was as if the light was not transmitted from the outside but enclosed within" (Pliny, *Natural History*, XXXVI, 163). From the vestibule, where the statue of Nero stood in the guise of the Sun-god Helios, the palace of the god must therefore have appeared "to shine like sparkling gold" before the on-looker (Seneca, *Moral Letters*, 115, 12).

After the death of Nero in AD 68, and precisely because of its unpopularity and the ideology that had inspired it – Otho and Vitellius used it briefly even though it was not complete – the *Domus Aurea* was literally swept away by the emperors who followed. On the Palatine, the Flavian Palace, which was planned by the architect Rabirius and inaugurated by Domitian in AD 92, erased the Neronian buildings and incorporated their foundations in the embankment created for the new palace. Already in Vespasian's reign the base of the *Domus Tiberiana* had been transformed to make space for a bath building with service rooms, while the central peristyle was transformed into a covered apsidal hall between the two lateral porticoes. In the valley the urban project of the Flavians planned to restore to the people the spaces occupied by the *Domus Aurea*, and led to the immediate destruction of Nero's buildings. The rooms that were destined to serve as a substructure for the terraces which connected the atrium to the lake (possibly never used) were cleared away and filled with rubble to allow for the raising of the land necessary for the construction of the Flavian amphitheatre.

This was inaugurated in AD 80 in the area previously occupied by the *stagnum Neronis* and its construction most probably meant that the front of the vestibule, which faced the valley, had to be moved back. Other Neronian structures were used below the walls of the *Meta Sudans*, dated between AD 80 and 96, while the porticoed road which rose from there towards the Palatine seems to have survived for many years. On the Velian hill, in AD 135, the emperor Hadrian dedicated the Temple of Venus and Rome which was built over the Neronian vestibule, and this might have influenced its layout. Already in Vespasian's reign, the vestibule had been opened to the public and the

Colossus, now dedicated to the Sun, was placed on the *via Sacra*. When Hadrian's temple was built, the statue was moved to an area nearer the amphitheatre—twenty-four elephants were used for its transportation. The Colossus went through modifications in Commodus' time: a representation of his own head as Hercules replaced the original, and the side support became a club. At his death, it went back to representing the Sun, with the right arm resting on a rudder. Destroyed perhaps during the first gothic invasions, the statue was remembered for the whole of the Middle Ages, and gave the name 'Coliseum' to the nearby amphitheatre. In 1933, in the valley of the Coliseum, the base of bricks which had supported it in the time of Hadrian was demolished. In AD 80, along the northern slope of the valley, the Baths of Titus were inaugurated, perhaps over an existing bath building connected with the *Domus Aurea*. The pavilion on the Oppian hill survived until AD 104, when it was damaged in a fire. Then the work for the construction of the great Baths of Trajan began on the summit of the hill. The architect Apollodorus of Damascus made use of Nero's building; it was filled up with earth and became an artificial substructure to widen the concrete bed of the baths, which were inaugurated in AD 109. Without light and turned into a subterranean complex, the palace on the Oppian hill owes its survival to Trajan's transformations.

9. "Vue d'une des exèdres des Thermes de Titus et de l'entrée des chambres souterraines", Mirri 1776

Nero

Lucius Domitius Ahenobarbus was born in AD 37 to Agrippina, sister of Caligula, and Gnaeus Domitius Ahenobarbus, a descendant of the triumvir Mark Anthony. He was adopted in AD 50 by the emperor Claudius, his mother's second husband. When Claudius died in AD 54, the Praetorian Guard acclaimed the 17 year-old Nero emperor, with the name Nero Claudius Drusus Germanicus Caesar. During the early years of his principate, Nero was under the influence of his tutors, the prefect Burrus and the philosopher Seneca, who represented the conservative tendencies of the Roman nobilitas. His policies were inspired by moderation and the example of Augustus, and tended towards the restoration of senatorial authority. This had been weakened by Claudius, who was guilty of according great power to the imperial freedmen and conceding the privileges of citizenship to too many provincials. Nero, who refused the title of 'father of the homeland', gave the impression of formally observing the ancient Republican establishment. He offered himself as mediator between the needs of the new classes and the acquired rights of the ancient ruling classes, and supported a clear separation between the administration of the private house of the princeps and that of the state. A series of acts of homage to the Senate and the passing of several laws—e.g. that which established an annual pension for senatorial families who had dissipated the wealth of the ancestors—seemed to contribute to the maintenance of the much heralded equilibrium.

While the assassination of Britannicus (AD 55), Claudius' son, and Nero's first wife Octavia, and also that of his mother Agrippina (AD 59) was acceptable, according to Seneca, to extirpate the legitimate descendants of Claudius and prevent meddling in the new imperial policies, the features of Nero's personality and his unwillingness to accept the control exercised by his tutors became rapidly obvious.

The Senate's refusal to accept a utopian abolition of indirect taxation which was thought up by Nero during that period, signalled the beginning of an open contrast between the powers of the state. This was exacerbated by the philhellenism of the emperor, which manifested itself in the introduction of solemn competitive displays to Rome.

Nero was immersed in his amateur passion for games, music and poetry, and the growth of a senatorial opposition induced him to seek the backing of the plebeians and also increase his prestige through military activity. The campaigns led by general Corbulo against the Parthians resulted in the recognition of the state of Armenia as Rome's vassal in AD 63. In the meantime, after the death of Burrus (AD 62), Seneca retired into private life, his policies having failed. In the same year, Nero murdered his wife Octavia, Claudius' daughter, who he had married in AD 53, and took as wife Poppea Sabina. She was to die, pregnant, in AD 65, perhaps because she had been kicked by the emperor himself. The following year, a new marriage to Statilia Messalina took place.

The cruelty of his personal policies, the fiscal pressure resulting from the pomp at the court, and the lese-majesty trials which were aimed at the confiscation of entire patrimonies, broadened the opposition to take in the plebeians too. In AD 64 a fire destroyed Rome, and despite the measures adopted in favour of the population which had suffered and a new town planning project which was to safeguard the city in the future, rumors arose that Nero himself had been responsible for the disaster. Nero himself accused the Christians, who underwent a cruel persecution). The enormous expenditure necessary for the reconstruction of the city and the new imperial residence – the Domus Aurea – sustained also by means of an extra levy asked of all the provinces, plus the monetary reform which meant the reduction of the weight of precious metal in coinage contributed to the growth of opposition and a collapse in Nero's popularity among the plebeians. The emperor's absolutist conception of power grew and he began to represent himself as the Sun, while the plot hatched by the opposition movement which had gathered around Gaius Calpurnius Piso failed because it was betrayed (AD 65). Among those who died in the bloodbath which followed were the philosopher Seneca and his nephew Lucan, the writer.

During a long visit to Greece in the following years (AD 66-67) the emperor even participated in the Isthmus games. Nero demagogically proclaimed the freedom of Greece; in practice merely a fiscal immunity, this measure increased the discontent of the other provinces. On his return to Rome (AD 68) he celebrated a great triumph, but the military crisis deepened rapidly. The insurrection led by Julius Vindex in the Gallic provinces was put down by Virginius Rufus; then senator Sulpicius Galba, governor of Hispania Tarraconensis rebelled, mostly due to the fiscal oppression. Nero was betrayed by the prefect of the praetorian guard who promised the soldiers a large gift on behalf of Galba. He was declared a public enemy by the Senate, while Galba was declared emperor. Having escaped to the villa of the freedman Phaon, a short distance from Rome, Nero had himself killed, at the age of 30, by the freedman Epaphroditus. According to tradition, his last words were: "What an artist perishes in me!"

The main sources for the history of Nero's principate—Tacitus (AD 54/55-120), Suetonius (AD 70-140) and Dio Cassius (AD 155-235)—all derive, directly and indirectly, from the political opposition and seem to be unanimously hostile to the emperor. Literary testimony and the Christian tradition, which soon identified Nero with Antichrist, have all contributed to the formation of the totally negative image of the emperor which has come down to us.

10. Portrait of Nero
dated between 59 and 64 AD
Rome, Palatine Museum

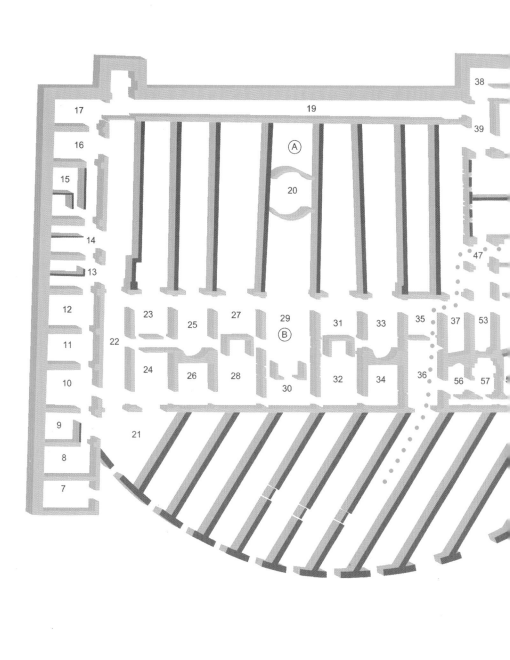

THE PAVILION
ON THE OPPIAN HILL

Severus and Celer: the architecture

Originally the pavilion stood in a dominant position on the southern slope of the Oppian hill, and was probably linked to the valley of the *stagnum Neronis* by a series of terraces.

The authors and executors of the project, the *magistri* and *machinatores*, were identified by Tacitus (*Annals*, XV, 42) as the architects Severus and Celer; we know nothing about them, not even their origins, except that they were the creators of the whole *Domus Aurea*.

The east-west orientation of the pavilion fitted into an artificial cut in the hill at a variable depth of between 30 and 60 metres. It faced the south and the valley, and had a façade which is currently documentable up to about 240 metres and was the front part of a complex which also occupied the summit of the hill, a second floor consisting of lightweight architecture and gardens. The palace survived for 35 years after the death of Nero and was briefly used by the emperor Otho, who gave "50 million sesterces for the completion of the *Domus Aurea*" (Suetonius, *Otho*, 7), and by his successor Vitellius. Galeria, his wife was not at all pleased with the imperial residence, considering it uncomfortable and undignified (Dio Cassius, LXV, 4). In AD 104 a fire destroyed part of the palace, and signalled the start of work for the construction of the Baths of Trajan on the top of the Oppian hill. The upper floor of the Neronian complex was knocked down and razed just above the floor level. The lower floor, stripped of all its precious materials and marble facings, was reinforced with large walls which divided the larger spaces up, creating a series of galleries covered with barrel vaults. All the openings on the outside were filled in and thus an enormous container full of earth and rubble was created, which artificially widened the concrete bed above.

On the terracing on the summit of the hill, Trajan's architect Apollodorus of Damascus constructed the bath complex, with a north-east/south-west orientation. For the first time, a separate area for living rooms and studios, with a large exhedra on the south-western side were added to the central block containing the baths themselves. This type of plan was to become the rule for later bath complexes. A great reservoir of water, known as the *Sette Sale*, but in fact made up of nine communicating parallel cisterns, preserves the alignment of Nero's pavilion, but is usually associated with the Baths of Trajan.

Buried underground, and crossed by main sewers of the baths

11. The vault of the Room of the owls (no. 29)

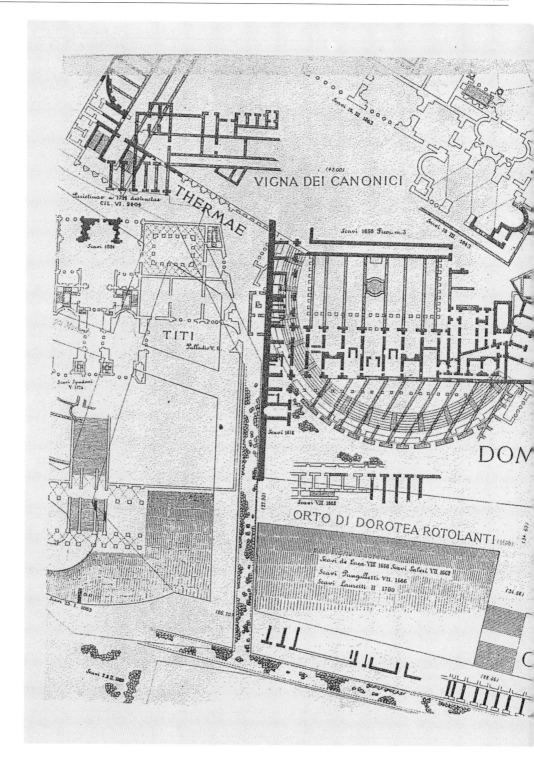

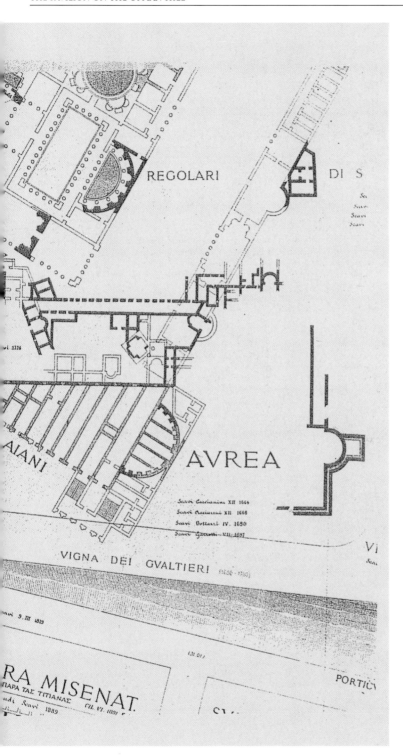

*12. Overall plan of the
pavilion on the Oppian hill
with Trajan's Baths above
in the Forma Urbis Romae
by Rodolfo Lanciani
(1893-1901), pl. 30*

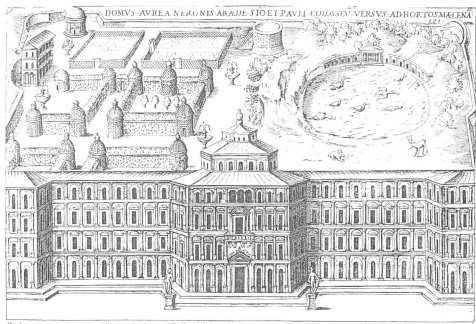

13. The Domus Aurea in an engraving by Giacomo Lauro (1612)

which perforated its vaults and walls, the palace on the Oppian hill remained hidden and was only rediscovered by visitors from the end of the 15th century onwards. Systematic excavation from the mid 18th century began to free the rooms from the enormous mass of earth which filled them, and a complex of 150 rooms has been recovered, of which 15 are still buried and 8 inaccessible; all are built in brick and covered mostly with barrel vaults of heights between 10 and 11 metres. Certain rooms have traces of a false ceiling. Therefore it is possible today to grasp the architectural greatness of the complex and the refinement of the decorative schemes, albeit very much degraded; however a fundamental element, the role played by light within the palace, is lost to us because of the superimposition of Trajan's Baths, which transformed the pavilion into an underground room. The sun filled the main rooms at the front of the building which faced south, penetrated into the rooms furthest from the peristyle or courtyards, lit up passageways and corridors from open windows in the walls and vaults, illuminated the marble facings, made the gold-leaf on the frescoes and stuccoes shine, created a play of light and reflected on the water of the fountains. The loss of this essential element forces the visitor today to try hard to imagine how it once was, which is fundamental to understand fully the greatness of the architectural invention, the refinement of the decorations of the palace and its symbolical value as the palace of the sun god Helios, i.e. Nero.

The whole of the west wing of the pavilion was preceded along

14. A gallery of Trajan's
in the courtyard-garden
of the western wing of the
Domus Aurea (no. 20):
at the centre the traces
of a fountain are visible

15. Eastern wing,
room no. 81: holes
from a counter-ceiling
carried out using
the cavity technique

the southern front by a single-pitch portico, which was perhaps Corinthian. The principal rooms opened on to this arcade, which probably ran along the whole side of the building
and faced the valley, receiving air and sun from south. The
whole appearance of the palace could not have differed much
from those "porticoed villas" which often appear in Pompeian
wall painting.

The pavilion on the Oppian hill can be divided into a western
area (from the western limit as far as the nymphaeum no. 45)
and an eastern area, representing two different architectural
conceptions. The western wing, which is almost totally ex-
cluded from the visit, presents a scheme of a type widespread
in the Roman world; it is organised around a courtyard-garden
(peristyle no. 20) along whose sides a series of rooms are
arranged. The peristyle is now divided into a series of parallel
galleries by the walls of Trajan's Baths. It has a statue base
against the northern wall and, in the middle, the impression of
a fountain. The porphyry cup now in the Rotonda del
Belvedere Vaticano may have come from here. To the north a
long cryptoporticus (no. 19), which may have been added at a
second stage, separated the complex from the hillside, while
on the other three sides the peristyle was surrounded by a portico, probably ionic.

The rooms discovered to the west (nos. 7-18) directly abut a
large containing wall which delimits the complex on this side,
while a double series of rooms on the southern side open onto
the peristyle and to the front of the palace alternately. The large
hall on the same axis as the courtyard (Room of the vault of the
owls, no. 29) was certainly meant for reception purposes, and
may have been a triclinium, while the nuclei of rooms placed
symmetrically at the sides are claimed—without much supporting evidence—to have had a private use as imperial apartments,
since two of the rooms (nos. 28 and 32) have quadrangular
niches thought to be recesses for beds. On the eastern side of the
peristyle, the vast hall (no. 44) may be one of the dining rooms
(*cenationes*) mentioned by Suetonius, or a living room (*oecus*) or
a winter triclinium. It opened originally by means of two colonnades onto the courtyard and towards a nymphaeum behind,
(no. 45) to great scenic effect. According to another interpretation, in origin room no. 44 must have had the form of an atrium with an impluvium. If this was the case, the whole western
wing of the palace would have taken on the characteristics of
those villas which, from the 2nd-3rd centuries BC combined the
Roman atrium with the Hellenistic garden-peristyle. It is in this
part of the western building that the only stairwell of the complex which leads to the upper floor has been found (no. 38).

The eastern wing, through which most of the visit takes place, has
a more innovative and articulated plan based around the octagonal
room complex (no. 128) and its radial rooms (nos. 122-126)
which create the symmetrical axis for the entire pavilion. The
rooms to the west of this are, in fact, arranged around a five-sided
courtyard, but the existence of a second identical symmetrical
courtyard to the east has been proven recently. If we assume that
the eastern part was identical in size to that of the western wing,
the whole building would have a length equal to about 370 metres.

16. The octagonal room (no. 128)

The main buildings of the eastern wing are arranged around the courtyard, —at the centre of which is the Room of the gilded vault (no. 80), perhaps a large triclinium—and along the front of the palace towards the valley. The service rooms and passageways are arranged in the rear. Along the cut made in the hillside, a series of corridors (nos. 19, 79, 92, 142) allowed a rapid communication between the different parts of the palace.

The incorporation of pre-existing structures into Nero's palace, result in anomalies and irregularities of the plan in certain areas of the eastern wing.

The upper floor of the pavilion, which was razed during Trajan's building work to a level of 30-60 centimetres above the floor, has been investigated in the area above the octagonal hall. Excavations have shown that the summit of the Oppian hill was occupied by porticoes and gardens, in which fountains and light-weight architecture were arranged, to judge from the slender walls which have come to light.

The area is bounded to the north and south by two porticoes, the first was above cryptoporticus 92, while the other, running between two apses, was above the portico on the lower floor which runs all the way along the façade of the pavilion. The area between the two porticoes was occupied to the south by walls which bounded the octagon of the room underneath; more to the north two rectangular fountains have come to light, which

17. Corridor (no. 79)
along the north side
of the eastern wing

have uneven borders which were originally veneered in marble, around which there are small rooms. At the sides of these fountain basins, two triangular impluvia which retraced the oblique sides of the courtyard on the lower floor.

In the northernmost part of the area under investigation, beyond the northern portico, there is a long canal (*euripus*) which has uneven borders and two apses at the sides, with a waterfall in the middle which flowed over the cryptoporticus 92 and emptied into the fountain of the nymphaeum in the octagonal room complex (no. 124).

On this upper floor there do not seem to be traces of those alterations and afterthoughts which characterised the lower floor

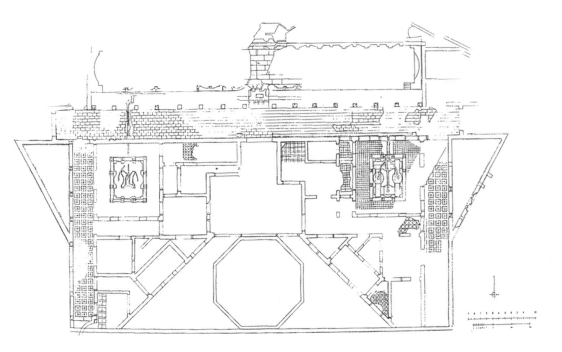

and which are a focus of the debate about the chronology of its different parts. If we assume that the entire pavilion was a single project, the rapidity of the execution, between AD 64 and 68, and the large number of workers employed would have led to anomalies, irregularities and readjustments during the work. In the whole complex we note passageways filled in, foundations excavated, and walls trimmed. However, some experts maintain that the construction of the western part was already underway from the time of the fire of AD 64 onwards and that it could even have been part of the *Domus Transitoria*.

But apart from a lack of proof, it has recently been demonstrated that the walls of the rooms behind nymphaeum 45, painted in fresco in Nero's time, were cut for the construction of the latter. Therefore, at least the nymphaeum would seem to belong to a later phase of the construction of the eastern area.

The difference in architectural conception between the two parts of the pavilion, the western area the more conservative, the eastern the more innovative, has also led to the theory that they were the works of two different architects, or that the intended use of the two wings of the palace were different, the first being the private apartments of the emperor, the second intended for public functions. According to recent studies, which tend to consider the pavilion not as an isolated building but part of the whole *Domus Aurea* complex, the palace never had a residential function. The number of doors opening inside the rooms, the lack of evidence for hinges on

18. Eastern wing: overall plan of the upper floor in the octagonal room area

*19. Rectangular fountain
and traces of the upper floor
of the pavilion
(Fabbrini excavations 1976)*

the doorjambs—even in the supposed bedrooms, which make one think of partial closures with curtains—, the lack of lavatories, kitchens and heating systems, the fact that it is impossible to identify a monumental entrance and that all the main rooms are accessible directly from the south facade, would lead us to rule out the possibility that the palace ever had residential features. In fact, what we have is a "dynamic" pavilion, inside which the emperor and his guests could walk, enjoying the space of the complex, its works of art, fountains, the panoramas looking over the park and the valley, and stopping in the main halls (Room of the vault of the owls, nymphaeum 45, Room of the gilded vault, octagonal room) given over to moments of repose.

The palace may not have been completed on the death of Nero; and with the work carried out by Otho and the transformations connected to the builders' yard for the Baths of Trajan, it began to lose the reception functions which had characterised it. The transformation of certain rooms, deprived of light, subdivided by partitions and intermediate floors, robbed of its marble veneer which was substituted by painted plaster work, carried out simply and hurriedly, altered the primitive grandeur of the complex. In the last period of its existence some parts probably had already been abandoned and others were being used as warehouses and service rooms related to the first construction work undertaken by Trajan.

Fabullus: the interior decoration

Evidence of the rich interior decoration of the *Domus Aurea*, the gold-leaf facings, gems, and fretted ivory ceilings, now consists merely of a memory passed down by the literary sources. Indeed, before transforming the pavilion into a gigantic substructure filled with earth, Trajan made sure that all the precious materials, including the marbles, were taken away. However, it is possible to reconstruct the decorative schemes of the walls by observing the traces left of the marble facings on the mortar beds. Orthostats (large rectangular slabs of polychrome marble) framed by cornices divided up by parastadae covered the walls of the most prestigious rooms, which were aligned with the peristyles and courtyards, up to the imposition of the vaults, on which the pictorial decoration lay, often enriched by stucco. The link between the height of the marble decoration and that of the frescoed surface seems to indicate a hierarchy in the importance of the rooms. Thus, while the rooms arranged around the main nuclei always have more marble facing than painting, it is painting which prevails above a socle of variable height in the connecting rooms, while it covers the entire wall in the service rooms arranged mainly towards the slope of the hill.

The polychrome marbles from the quarries of Greece, Asia Minor, Africa were used not only in the wall-decoration, but also in the floors and veneer of baths and water slides. They were illuminated by the light which filled the rooms, and must have been a sign of the pomp and wealth consistent with the grandiose nature of the architectural inventiveness. The lively polychromy of the decorative scheme, the intense red of Tae-

20. *Room of the vault of the owls (no. 29): the traces left by the marble veneer are clearly visible on the mortar bed*

21. *Room no. 73: traces of an opus sectile floor*

narus marble or the red spotted with porphyry white, the green of Serpentine, the yellow of Numidian marble, the white of pentelic or the violet streaks of Pavonazzetto, the pink of Portasanta can only to be imagined today on the basis of rare fragments which have come to light inside the monument.

The same materials must have been used in the floors where, in certain cases, the only element preserved is the white marble of the doorstones.

Even the floors were completely stripped in Trajan's reign, but on the mortar beds in some rooms we can see the traces of marble cut into rectangular slabs (nos. 29, 44 and 45) or into geometric forms juxtaposed to form a polychrome design using the technique called *opus sectile* (no. 73). Only four rooms, certainly of secondary importance, preserve floor mosaics, made up of small white tesserae (nos. 72 and 77), in some cases decorated with black tessera in geometric motifs (nos 114-116). The refinement of the marble facings was paralleled by that of the pictorial decoration which covered the top part of the walls and vaults. Carried out with a fresco technique, it is usually classified as part of the initial phase of the so-called "fourth Pompeian style". This is a decorative system inspired by stage settings which divides the walls with slender and complex architectural elements (almost without any structural value); illusory perspective backgrounds are enriched with a vast repertory of ornamental and fantastic motifs, small landscape pictures, fabric motifs, all carried out with a pronounced pictorial and impressionistic sense.

According to the literary tradition, the painter responsible for the decoration of the *Domus Aurea* was Fabullus (called Famulus or Amulius in a variety of Plinian codexes). Thus Pliny says: "Also the painter Famulus lived a short while ago, grave and severe and at the same time florid and humid. The Minerva is his work, which looked at the spectator from whatever direction he observed it. He painted only a few hours a day, but this also with solemnity, always dressed in a toga, even on the scaffolding. The *Domus Aurea* was like the prison of his art: outside, he didn't do much work" (Pliny, *Natural History,* XXXV, 120).

The first two terms used by Pliny, "grave and severe", must have referred to the personality of this artist, the courtly and aristocratic nature of his painting which is symbolised by his painting in a toga, and which perhaps alludes also to his choice of mythological themes. The other two adjectives, "florid and humid", characterise his technique of painting.

Pliny makes a distinction between austere and florid colours: "florid—and it is the patron who supplies them for the painter, at his own expense: red lead paint, *Armenium, cinnabaris,* chrysocolla, indigo and *purpurissum,* the others are austere" (Pliny, *Natural History,* XXXV, 30). Later he says that of all the colours supplied to the painter by the patron it is "purpurissum above all" which is the most expensive (Pliny, *Natural History,* XXXV, 44). The term 'florid' therefore indicates the rich use of colour by the painter, who uses florid colours, common inside the *Domus Aurea*: cinnabar red, the azure extracted from azurite, dark red, green, indigo, and pur-

22. Painted wall of the Room of the black vault (no. 32), Mirri 1776

ple, the most precious, taken from the colouring material extracted from shells of the *Murex* species. The term 'humid' might indicate the pastiness and fluidity of Fabullus' technique and the management of colour in painting.

In reality, at least two different artistic trends can be distinguished inside the *Domus Aurea*. In the western wing above the marble socle the pictorial decoration is currently in a ruined state but is known from Renaissance and 18th century copies; here the painting is carried out in two bands: the lower tends to reproduce walls enclosed within their actual limits, decorated with large closed monochrome panels, prevalently in black, red and dark yellow, in the middle of which miniature paintings are suspended. In the upper band and in the lunettes the wall opens on to an imaginary background by means of slender architectural motifs in perspective. What characterises the decorative systems of this part of the pavilion is the fineness of detail of the painted decorative elements. The use of stucco is limited to the cornices and slender figurines on monochrome backgrounds. Plant spirals, linear elements transformed in to floral garlands, subtle candelabra, motifs taken from textile craftsmanship, highlighted with abundant use of gold-leaf, divide the wall with elegant care, recalling the Hellenistic method of hanging figured tapestry. The partitions of the walls are in fact to be compared to the description of the festive tent of the Egyptian king Ptolemy II Philadelphus, in which a banquet was held during a festive procession in c. 279 BC. The tent was divided into sections by fabrics stretched between fluted balusters. In the middle of these tapestries hung small figured pictures (*pinakes*), which reproduced famous paintings (Athenaeus, V, p. 196a, 25 f.).

Indeed, by imitating a Hellenistic tent as seen from the inside, the whole repertoire of decorative elements was repeated in an infinite number of possible combinations on the vaults, and were also predominant in the figured scenes. The vault of the main hall, aligned with the long side of the peristyle (Vault of the Owls, no. 29), is divided by a series of friezes articulated around the central figured painting, in which plant motifs abound, as well as masks alternating with palmettes, fantastic animals, hanging drapery, draped herms growing out of plant candelabra, shields, marine monsters, dolphins facing each other, all arranged in an unending series of decorative bands. The frieze, which gives its name to the ceiling, consists of owls on floral corollas alternated with images of Minerva. These are broken up by circular medallion friezes, upon which figurines in stucco stand out, and as small landscape pictures. Along the central axes and the diagonals of the ceiling plant-like candelabra converge towards the central panel, supporting medallions of different forms with stucco figures inside. The inspiration for the so-called "yellow vault" (no. 31) is once more the motif of the tent and the fabrics, which are articulated around a central medallion and subdivided by bands of red colour in panels replete with decorative motifs. The theme of suspended drapery returns in the vault with the red background in room no. 33, along with an infinite series of friezes full of animal fig-

23. The Yellow Vault (no. 31) in an engraving by Nicolas Ponce (1786)

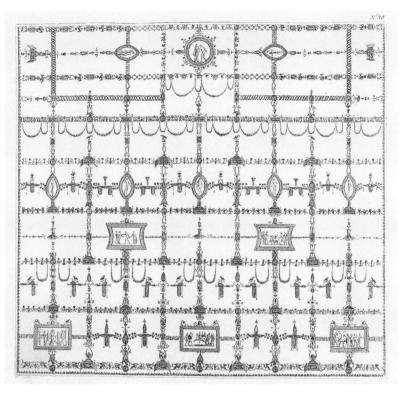

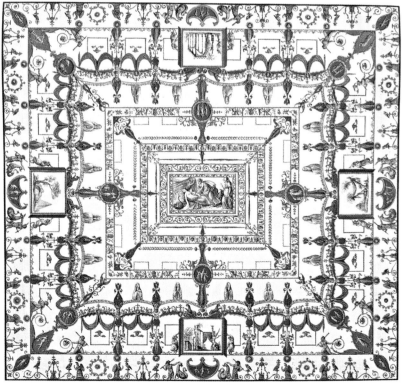

ures and plant elements, small hanging figured paintings crowned with trophies of winged genii. In room 32 garlands, floral wreaths, palmettes, medallions of different forms spread out on the black background.

In the eastern section the walls are decorated with architectural divisions in which the stucco, coloured and faced with gold-leaf, often becomes the skeleton for the perspective which opens out on to a painted illusionistic backgrounds: fluted balusters, parastadae, cornices, relief entablatures frame the fields in which figures are arranged on the various levels (see, among others, room nos. 41, 42, 74, 119 and 129). Complex polychrome façades, carried out without stucco, painted on a light background to give the impression of space, crowded with characters, enriched by garlands and hanging drapery, decorate – with a taste which owes something to theatre scenes – some of the neighbouring rooms of the main nuclei (nos. 70 and 131). The ceilings of the most important rooms (nos. 80, 119, 129) are divided by elaborate frames in stucco, enriched with colour and, once, by gold leaf, in geometric patterns which enclose the figured paintings.

A different artistic style is reserved for the rooms of secondary importance and corridors. Complex friezes of animal and plant characters or architectural divisions which are linear but insubstantial, once more divided on two or three bands and painted on a light background, enclose small paintings of a sacred nature or lakes in the Hellenistic tradition or simple still-lifes, and are crowded with a vast repertory of images made up

24. The Black Vault (no. 32) in an engraving by Nicolas Ponce (1786)

25. The Vault of the Owls (no. 29), Mirri 1776

26. The Vault of the Owls (no. 29): detail of the pictorial decoration as it is at the moment

of figurines, marine monsters, floral elements, animals, masks, vases, all treated with rapid blotched brushstrokes. Linear architectural motifs are also to be found on the ceilings of the corridors (no. 92), often subdivided into areas, each decorated with its own motifs, which assume the appearance of painted fabrics.

In general, as far as the decorated divisions of ceilings and walls are concerned, it is obvious that at least two workshops, linked with two different artistic trends, were operating inside the pavilion. They were divided more or less into eastern and western areas, even though the problem of whether they were contemporary or not has not yet been resolved. While some scholars see a logical evolution developing from the painting of the western area, which are considered still to be linked to the courtly and neoclassical so-called "third Pompeian style", leading to the "fourth style" carried out in the eastern area, others claim the opposite. According to the latter the architectural motifs in the west wing are a re-elaboration of those present in the eastern area. What is certain is that the two workshops were working almost at the same time and that, as has been noted, both are characterised by a taste for miniature detail which, since it can only be perceived close-up, seems not at all worthy of the architectonic greatness of the rooms. Probably this meant that craftsmen used to decorating much smaller rooms had to extend their habitual decorative schemes over the vaster surfaces of Nero's pavilion.

27. The Room of Achilles at Scyros (no. 119): detail of the painted "fourth style" decoration, with stucco architectural elements

Although the decorative schemes are still visible today, it is much more difficult to analyse the themes reproduced in the figured paintings, which must have formed the ideological basis for the decoration of the *Domus Aurea*. Those from the western area have completely disappeared, but have been partially reproduced, with a certain liberty of positioning and interpretation, in 18th century copies. There seems to be an abundance of subjects linked to Bacchus (Bacchus and Ariadne, Ariadne abandoned by Theseus, the Birth of Bacchus, the Child Bacchus delivered to the nymphs, Bacchus and the four seasons). These dionysiac scenes, together with the painting representing the child Hercules brought by Zeus to the breast of Hera asleep—perhaps painted on the Vault of the Owls—and the central painting of the golden vault with Zeus carrying off Ganymede to take him to the sky to be cupbearer of the gods, are all subjects linked to themes of initiation, which promise a rebirth to the initiated. The allusion to the new golden age promised to humanity during the principate of Nero is obvious.

In the eastern wing of the palace we also see figured paintings on the ceilings of room 119 (*Achilles and the daughters of Lycomedes in Scyros*) and room 129 (*Hector's farewell to Andromache on the walls of Troy* and a scene of uncertain interpretation, which may be the meeting between Paris and Helen or the myth of Protesilaus and Laodamia). Episodes taken from the Trojan cycle also decorated the ceiling of a room on the Palatine, related to the *Domus Transitoria*, which have been attributed by

28. Room no. 131: detail of the painted decoration with false architecture peopled with figures

*29. Room no. 80: division
into geometric fields
on the gilded vault*

all to Fabullus himself. Here, too, the subjects can be linked to Nero's ideology: the emperor is the one who, from the ruins of the fire, will create a new Troy. It is difficult to say which part of the decoration of the pavilion is by Fabullus. If we rule out the painting in the rooms of secondary importance and the architectonic façades— indeed, the artist is defined by Pliny as a painter and not as author of decorative schemes—we tend to attribute to him, as well as the painting of the *Domus Transitoria*, at least the grandiose decoration of the gilded ceiling and those scenes which indicate a vast range of colour and a dynamic composition, such as the painting of Achilles at Scyros.

In the decoration of the pavilion on the Oppian hill there is also the wall mosaic which covered ceilings (nos. 44 and 124) and extended over friezes (nos. 44 and 45). The only mosaic left is that which occupies the central octagon on the ceiling of nymphaeum 45, which represents Ulysses holding out the goblet of wine to Polyphemus, the first example of a mosaic with a figured subject on a ceiling.

30. Cryptoporticus no. 92: linear type painted decoration

31. The same, detail of the vault decoration with rectangles animated by figurines in the watercolour by F. Weege (1913)

THE WORKS OF ART

The grandiose architectural inventiveness and the sumptuousness of the decorative schemes in the *Domus Aurea* were suitably accompanied by a large number of works of art. Nero's philhellenism did not stop him from unashamedly pillaging most of these works from Greece (Pausanias, X, 27, 3-5). Pliny, after listing the names of famous bronze sculptors and their works, states "all the most famous are today in Rome, dedicated by the emperor Vespasian in the Temple of Peace and the other buildings he had erected; brought to Rome after the brutal pillaging of Nero, they were arranged in the halls of the *Domus Aurea*" (Pliny, *Natural History*, XXXIV, 84).

Among the sculptures possessed by the emperor, Pliny mentions a statue of Amazon, by Strongylion, most probably from Athens, and a portrait of Alexander the Great carried out by Lysippus, perhaps the Alexander with the spear, erected at Ephesus in 334 BC, which Nero had gilded and which perhaps was preserved on the Palatine (Pliny, *Natural History*, XXXIV, 48, 62, 83).

Recently it has been suggested that the *dying Galatian* and the *Galatian killing himself and his wife* were placed inside the octagonal room. The two works were part of a group related to the donarium of Attalus I in Pergamum, erected by Epigonos to commemorate the victory over the Galatians, which took place around 230 BC. The bronze originals remained in Pergamum up till AD 64, when Nero had them brought to Rome and placed in the *Domus Aurea* (Pliny, *Natural History*, XXXIV, 84). The statues are known from copies in Asiatic marble, perhaps carried out in Pergamum itself around the mid-1st century BC and rediscovered in Rome c. 1620 during the construction of Villa Ludovisi. It is probable that they were transferred to Rome to commemorate the Gallic victories of Caesar (46-43 BC) and exhibited inside the *Horti Sallustiani*, which at that time were owned by Caesar himself.

An analysis of the bases has shown that the figures belonged to a single group, which represented the human drama of the defeated barbarians, and were preserved in Pergamum on a circular (or rectangular according to another theory) base.

The excavations inside the pavilion on the Oppian hill have brought to light only the statue of a Muse, possibly part of a group deriving from an original by Praxiteles which the consul Lucius Mummius had transported to Rome in 146 BC. But it is once again Pliny who informs us of the famous Laocoön group "which is in the house of the emperor Titus, a work to be admired above any painting or any bronze statue: Laocoön, his

32. Lawrence Alma-Tadema,
A Sculpture Gallery in Rome
at the Time of Augustus, 1867.
Montreal, Musée des Beaux-Arts

*33. A Galatian killing himself
and his wife.
Rome, Museo Nazionale Romano
in Palazzo Altemps*

*34-35. Dying Galatian.
Rome, Capitoline Museums*

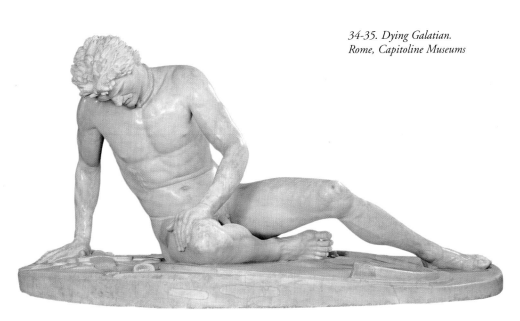

sons and the marvellous tangles of the serpents, were sculpted in the same marble along the lines of a common project, by remarkable artists: Agesander, Polydorus and Athenodorus from Rhodes" (Pliny, *Natural History*, XXXVI, 37). A tradition which grew up in the 17th century which placed the discovery of the Laocoön inside the room of Hector and Andromache, but actually the group came to light in 1506, that is when during the Renaissance visits to the "grottoes" were at their most intense, in a vineyard near the *Sette Sale*, inside a room situated in that sector of the *Domus Aurea* used by the emperor Titus. The room must then have been attached to the Baths of Trajan (that the Laocoön was buried after the fire of AD 104 does not seem feasible) and was probably buried in the 6th century, after the entire complex had been abandoned. The statuary group represents the priest who denounced the Trojan horse to the hesitant Trojans and was killed, with one or both of his sons—depending on the version of the story—by two serpents which appeared suddenly. It has been considered by some to be an original of the mid-Hellenistic age, similar in terms of the complexity of style and arrangement to the Pergamum school. But in actual fact the Laocoön seems to be from Tiberius' reign: the three Rhodian sculptors mentioned by Pliny are also the authors of the group with Scylla, Ulysses and Polyphemus, discovered in the grotto of Tiberius in Sperlonga. The area where it was discovered was probably part of the interior of the *Horti* of Maecenas, later attached to the *Domus Aurea*, where Tiberius had lived from AD 2 to 14.

The discovery of the Laocoön made a big impression and exercised a great deal of influence on 16th century art—we need only recall the sculpture of Michelangelo's mature years. Indeed, Vasari refers to how a particular 'dry manner, crude and rough' encountered in art until that time was overcome by "seeing certain old things excavated from the earth, that were discussed in Pliny, among the most famous the Laocoön, Hercules and the large torso of the Bel Vedere, the Cleopatra, the Apollo and many others" (G. Vasari, *Lives*, third part, Preface).

REDISCOVERY

The "Renaissance Grotesques" and eighteenth century copies
The abandonment of the Baths of Trajan, probably because the aqueducts were cut in AD 539 by Vitigis, king of the Ostrogoths, led to the beginning of a profound transformation of the Oppian *hill* and for the whole of the Middle Ages it would be covered with gardens and vineyards. The memory of the *Domus Aurea* was lost for centuries and the underground ruins were only rediscovered towards the end of the 15th century, when large numbers of visitors began to lower themselves down into the underground "grottoes". They began to copy and then circulate the decorative motifs of the vaults, which inspired the invention and the widespread popularity of the "grotesques" in the art of the day. "…These grotesques were named as such by contemporaries because they were found in certain caverns of the earth, which in antiquity were rooms, ovens, studios, halls and other things like this" (B. Cellini, *Life*, Florence 1568, ed. P. D'Ancona, p. 70).
Many holes had opened up as parts of the complex caved-in; once they had been lowered into the pavilion, the visitors walked on the infill—which at that time reached to the vaults—and penetrated from one room to another, opening passages in the upper sections of the walls. These breaches, together with the numbers of signatures traced in soot or scratched on the paintings and the collections of drawings of decorative motifs which were well-known at the end of the 15th century, allow us to identify which rooms were visited during the Renaissance. In the eastern wing, the visitors reached the radial rooms of the octagonal hall (nos. 122-126) and the Room of Hector and Andromache (no. 129). Corridor 79 and cryptoporticus 92, and their adjacent rooms, seem to have been among the places most visited, together with the Room of the gilded vault (no. 80) which must have been directly accessible from the top of the Oppian hill. In the western area the rooms visited during the Renaissance were the Room of the vault of the owls (no. 29), the Room of the yellow vault (no. 31) and the Room of the black vault (no. 34). Room no. 33 was found much later.
Among the many visitors who discovered by torchlight the world populated by the fantastic beings of Nero's paintings, were a number of Tuscan and Umbrian artists, such as Ghirlandaio, Pinturicchio, Perugino and Filippino Lippi, all of whom had been called to Rome c. 1480 by Sixtus IV to decorate the Sistine Chapel. They were particularly struck by the decorative motifs of the *Domus Aurea* which seemed to them to be a pure expression of the freedom of imagination. In the 16th

37. Giovanni da Udine (1487-1564), detail of the decoration of a pilaster of the Vatican Logge century, Vasari explained: "The grotesques are a very licentious and ridiculous type of painting, done by the ancients to adorn rooms... and those who created the strangest designs were considered the best" (*Lives*, Preface, *On painting*, ch. XVII). Already by the mid-15th century, this taste for monstrous figures, an inheritance of the gothic period, crowded pilasters, architraves and friezes with overwhelming decoration, and fed an interest in the fantastic motifs copied from the rooms of the *Domus Aurea* which could be combined to form endless variations. This first generation of artists who had frequented Nero's "grottoes" were still influenced by 15th century taste, and in their reproduction of motifs tended to arrange them symmetrically with respect to a middle axis. Fantastic monochrome candelabra were created and painted on columns, which framed figured scenes, or on buildings in scenes for which they were the background.

In the last decades of the 15th century, candelabra with grotesques decorated the backgrounds, columns and friezes of architecture painted by Ghirlandaio. These are arranged with an endless variety of motifs on the *logge* which appear in the paintings of Pinturicchio, where the rapid brushstrokes and the bright colours show the profound influence Neronian models. They fill the corbels and cells of vaults which are divided up by cornices into geometric fields in imitation of those of the *Domus Aurea*. In the work of Filippino Lippi and Signorelli they tend to invade walls with complex illusionistic backgrounds.

Many of these artists frequented the ruins of the pavilion personally. Pinturicchio's signature is scratched in the painting of the yellow vault (no. 31), and he copied motifs from the Vault of the Owls. Some of the archaeological drawings by Filippino Lippi seem to refer to Nero's palace. Ghirlandaio signed his name in the Room of Hector and Andromache (no. 129), and was prob-

38. Domenico Ghirlandaio (1449-1494), The Birth of Mary. Florence, Choir-stalls, Santa Maria Novella

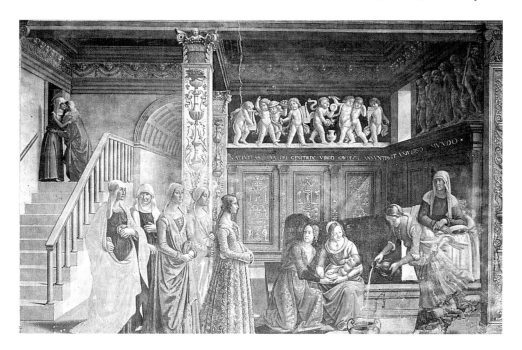

ably the author of a series of sketches which he used to derive a
collection of drawings containing motifs copied in the *Domus
Aurea* (*Codex Escurialensis*) and dated around 1494. The possibility of copying motifs from what amounted to authentic note-
books led, at the beginning of the 16th century, to the spread of
grotesques outside Rome and their use in sculpture, ceramics,
and the decoration on palace façades. Soon there were specialists
in grotesques, above all the craftsmen in Pinturicchio's workshop
in Rome, although they did not always draw from a repertoire
taken directly from archaeological prototypes. It is with Raphael's
workshop—above all the in the work of Giovanni da Udine—
that grotesque decoration abandoned 15th century schemes once
and for all, and began to cover entire areas with complete imita-
tions of Nero's rooms. Raphael was a frequent visitor to the ruins of the *Domus Aurea* (his signature can be read in cryptoporticus 92); Vasari claims that Raphael was first taken to see the
"grottoes" by the Friuli painter, where both were struck by the
beauty and freshness of the painting and stuccoes.

The first room to be entirely covered with decoration taken
from ancient models was the *Stufetta* (bathroom), painted by
Giovanni da Udine between 1513 and 1515 in the Vatican
apartments of Cardinal Bibbiena. This was probably one of
Raphael's projects, and has a red background in imitation of the
cinnabar on Roman walls. The painting consists of three bands:
the lowest contains panels with a black background and small
scenes of cupids seemingly derived from Pompeian frescoes and

*39. Pinturicchio (1454-1513),
Annunciation. Spello,
Santa Maria Maggiore,
Cappella Baglioni*

40. The Stufa of Cardinal
Bibbiena. Rome, Vatican Palaces

figured paintings illustrating stories of Venus. The upper part of the wall has fantastic architectural settings: slender pavilions, decorated with garlands and hung drapery, enclose winged cupids, while in the centre, above the wall recesses, delicate figurines are arranged inside small paintings with black backgrounds, in imitation of the stucco figurines of Neronian painting. The vault is divided into geometric fields containing figured scenes and figurines of animals, and is similar to the ceilings of the Oppian hill pavilion in its overall structure.

Still under the direction of Raphael, Giovanni da Udine, together with Perin del Vaga, Giulio Romano and others, participated in the decoration of the Vatican Logge, i.e. the great arcade next to the papal apartment, on the second floor of the Vatican palaces which was finished in 1519. Here, the composition seems to return to 15th century schemes; the grotesques are confined to the columns and semi-pilasters of the *Loggia* which divide the background wall, and are arranged symmetrically in a reprisal of the candelabra motif. There is an elegance and a greatness never before achieved. The surfaces are enriched with stucco medallions in which figurines, small scenes and still-lifes are arranged in white on a coloured background. The sequence of the medallions seems to be inspired directly by the black vault of the *Domus Aurea*, but the animals, plant decorations, and other objects which are inserted into Giovanni da Udine's grotesque decoration are unlike the typical style of Neronian painting and evolve towards a marked naturalism. There is a realistic imitation of plants and animals, of objects arranged to form trophies, the transformation of the decorative elements of the grotesques into authentic still-lifes which are free from archaeological models (though these still influence the design).

The *Loggetta* of the apartment of Bibbiena, which was planned by Raphael and decorated by Giovanni da Udine with Perin del Vaga, perhaps has a later date than the *Logge*, but is closer to the ancient model. It was inspired by the great cryptoporticus of the Domus Aurea and has a partition of the walls on three levels, where the grotesques stand out on a clear background. On a decorated socle with geometric motifs, the internal wall alternates painted recesses containing female figures and panels with small paintings—scenes of the Apollo and Marsyas cycle—in the centre. The whole of the wall and the lunettes are covered with slender architectural motifs from which hang festoons, garlands and fabric drapery; these are covered with cupids, monstrous beings, every type of animal, bird, trophy, and object. At the centre, the vault reflects the carpet decoration of cryptoporticus 92, albeit in a more simplified version, and, as in the Neronian model, it is covered with fantastic slender architectural motifs, with pavilions enclosing divinities. The paintings in the *Loggetta* on the whole show a meticulous imitation of ancient models, but once more the treatment of the plant and animal motifs have a naturalism which is not found in Neronian painting.

Throughout the whole of the 16th century, the decoration of *Logge* opening on to parks and gardens is characterised by grotesques painted on a clear background, enlivened by pergo-

41. Vatican Logge, detail of a newel

42. Vatican Logge

las, garlands and festoons. The combination of painting and stucco returns in the loggia of Villa Madama in Rome, finished after the death of Raphael by Giovanni da Udine, Giulio Romano and Baldassarre Peruzzi. We owe to Peruzzi a series of decorations of *Logge*, carried out c. 1520, in which linear architectural motifs enclose figures, animals and birds on a white background.

In 1527, the sack of Rome by Charles V caused the dispersal of the artists who had gathered around Raphael's workshop; but the ruins of the *Domus Aurea* continued to be visited until the last years of the 16th century, when signatures traced in blood appear on the paintings. Then in the 17th century the signatures disappear for good.

Renewed interest in Roman antiquity in the mid 18th century

led to a reprisal of visits to the pavilion, as is documented by the first signatures in pencil lead. It is to this period that a new series of copies of the paintings of the *Domus Aurea*—at the time mistaken for the Baths of Titus—belong. These consist of sixty engravings, derived from drawings by Smugliewicz and Brenna, and were published in 1776 by the Roman antiquary Mirri with a commentary by the abbot Carletti. The engravings reproduce the decorative schemes of vaults and walls (Mirri himself had sixteen rooms cleared) and show the great imagination and freedom of interpretation of the copies with respect to the originals (where these can seen be seen). The artists themselves mention alterations and additions made during the work, to which we should add errors of interpretation. A few years later, in 1786, the Frenchman Nicholas Ponce published a series of engravings which were taken from Mirri, and made modifications by inverting scenes, substituting certain elements with others, and adding details. Despite the freedom of interpretation shown by the copiers and the inaccuracies also concerning the localisation of the rooms, the 18th century copies are fundamental for an understanding of the overall aesthetic conception of Neronian painting.

*43. Perugino (1448-1523),
Storie di San Bernardino:
The Healing of the Young Woman
Perugia, Galleria Nazionale
dell'Umbria*

THE VISIT

From the start of the visit, it is immediately obvious that Trajan's Baths were constructed over Nero's pavilion. The partially restored façade which makes up the lower part of the southeastern hemicycle of the baths is today the monumental entrance of the *Domus Aurea*. The curved elevation is pierced by a series of passageways and arcades which are matched by windows above, enriched with small projecting arches and supported by travertine corbels.

In the garden before the entrance a number of structures maintain the alignment of Nero's palace, and are dated by brickstamps to the Hadrianic age. The limited remains of the floors are to be found at the same level as the ground floor of Trajan's galleries.

At the end of the entrance lane, a small building which once formed part of Nero's palace was transformed into a Christian oratory, dedicated to Santa Felicita. The remains of wall-paintings were discovered inside this building in 1812; drawings were carried out at the time of their discovery, but today only two copies are preserved. One is now in the collections of the Kircherian Museum in the Museo Nazionale Romano in Rome and the other at the Vatican library. The main fresco was a scene in which Santa Felicita, with her seven children around her, receives the crown of precious stones, the symbol of beatified immortality, from God, which she earned by her martyrdom under Marcus Aurelius. Martyrs were solemnly celebrated in the Christian calendar on the 10th July.

The palace is reached through one of the galleries which, like all Trajanic structures, was buried to create the robust foundations of the bath building. These galleries were not originally given any type of wall facing and the cement nucleus of their barrel vault covering and their unplastered wall in brick or mixed brick and tufa can be clearly seen. Inside, a series of photographic panels have been set up for the visit.

In the right hand corner at the end of the gallery, below the level of the pavement today, we can see the foundations on which stands the plinth of a column from a portico, perhaps of a Corinthian order, which formed the facade of the western wing towards the valley. It can be seen from the beam-holes in the facade at the western end of the building that the portico had a single sloped roof; here there is also another column base.

We enter Nero's residence by changing direction: the Golden House is planned according to cardinal points, but Trajan's

44. Corridor "of the eagles" (no. 50): detail of the decoration of the vault with the eagles on a shield and winged gryphons

45. Substructure of Trajan's exhedra which represents the present-day entrance to the Domus Aurea

building has a NE/SW orientation in order to take full advantage of the light and heat of the sun. This was to be repeated in all later bath buildings in Rome.

Nero's palace is today covered by the Oppian hill gardens. Liberated from the 17th century onwards from the earth which filled it, the interior of the palace has suffered from microclimate variations, caused by the infiltration of water and variations in the level of humidity. These factors are responsible not only for the crystallisation of salts on the frescoed surfaces—which leads to calcium deposits on the paintings, as can be seen on the vault of the first room (no. 35)—but also for biological attack, the formation of algae, fungi and moss. The itinerary begins in the western part of the palace (rooms nos. 35 and 36), which is organised around the large rectangular courtyard-garden (peristyle no. 20). Of the series of rooms which look out on to the southern side of the peristyle, interpreted by some as the private apartments of the emperor, only the perspective of the sequence of the doors with their brick lintels can be grasped. The visit continues to the right, to room no. 37 where the last remaining part of the peristyle (no. 20) can be seen on the left. This was transformed into a gallery by Trajan. On the wall at the end, which separates the open space from cryptoporticus no. 19, there is a fresco with large black panels bordered in red; here evidence for the roof of the portico (perhaps of an ionic order) which surrounded the courtyard on three sides can also be seen. On the other side a *cocciopesto* floor of white rhombs stands out among the few remains of masonry which relate to the residential quarter of private houses which had begun growing up on the Oppian hill during the Republican age but was destroyed in the fire of AD 64.

46. Corridor no. 50 or "of the eagles", detail with birds facing each other at the sides of a plant candelabra

The following rooms (nos. 47, 48, 49), which in the original plan were in direct communication with room 44, have been through successive transformations. In the last phase of the life of the palace, after the passageways were closed off, a very simple pictorial decoration of linear partitions on a white background was laid out over the blocked doors and the rest of walls; this happened before the pavilion became a substructure of Trajan's baths and the vaults of neighbouring rooms were reinforced (nos. 53, 54 and 55) with large brick arches.

A richer decorative scheme characterises corridor no. 50, called "of the eagles" Inside the outer band, which runs around the vault, the rectangular fields present eagles spreading their wings over medallions, at the sides of which there are two griffins. Stucco caryatids and painted tripods separate the panels alternately. The decoration of the ceiling, unfortunately almost completely lost, is known from 18th century engravings.

A second frieze, adorned with vegetation, enclosed the central rectangle which was subdivided into panels. At the two extremities of the shorter sides there was a scene of a sacrifice and a pastoral scene, while the rectangle hosted the main picture. A virile nude figure with a helmet and spear seems to be descending from the heavens and turns his eyes towards a sleeping woman and two minor characters. According to De Romanis, scholars identified this painting as the discovery and seduction of Rhea Silvia by the god Mars, giving an insignificant role to the other two figures. However, a closer examination carried out in 1982 by Yves Perrin linked the four characters to the myth of Ariadne after she had been abandoned by Theseus, who is protected by the *genius* of sleep in the presence of Minerva. An error of interpretation by the copyst must have transformed Minerva into a male figure. The plaster on the wall reaches down to the floor; above architectonic perspectives divided by slender balusters, fluted in stucco are arranged on two superimposed levels.

The rest of corridor no. 50 communicates with rooms 44 and 45, which form the nymphaeum complex.

The nymphaeum of Ulysses and Polyphemus

This is one of the most impressive parts of the whole pavilion on the Oppian hill; but it is difficult to interpret correctly because of the alterations carried out during the short lifespan of the palace before the transformations under Trajan.

The complex is made up of three rooms conceived as a single project with a unified architectural prospective: hall no. 44, the nymphaeum of Ulysses and Polyphemus (no. 45), and a cross wing. The large hall no. 44, inserted between the peristyle (no. 20) and the nymphaeum (no. 45), originally had its two short sides divided by two porticoes of four columns each. These created a sort of partition through which the eye passed on its way to the water display in the room situated at the end (no. 45), which formed the focus of the perspective. It is uncertain whether hall no. 44 had an open roof or had been covered with barrel vaults with a width of 13.50 metres, for which the attachments are visible, buttressed by three perpendicular rooms on each of the sides.

The light must have played a fundamental role, increasing the visual effect of the complex. It penetrated from the peristyle (no. 20) through the porticoes of hall no. 44, flooded into the intermediate corridor, which perhaps remained unroofed, and was reflected in the water of the nymphaeum (no. 45) after passing through the windows which, at the time, opened on to the small side courtyards (nos. 43 and 51). This original plan was completely transformed when a brick wall with only three doors surmounted by three windows, still visible today, substituted the colonnade which led to the nymphaeum

47. Decoration of the vault of corridor no. 50 or "of the eagles", Mirri 1776

48. Perspective view of the nymphaeum of Ulysses and Polyphemus complex from peristyle no. 20

E.PAPARAITI '93

in hall no. 44, almost completely obscuring the perspective vision of this sequence of rooms. At the same time, the nymphaeum itself was further deprived of light when six windows were transformed into niches, intended perhaps for statues, and the two doors in the intermediate corridor which had led into the two small side courtyards were blocked up. Although they were architecturally separated after these works, the three rooms of the complex received a unified decoration in this new phase. Marble had been arranged on the floors in rectangular slabs (the imprints of which can still be seen); now it also covered the walls up to the mosaic frieze. This frieze ran under the vault and was bordered by a reddish band enclosed within two lines of white tesserae, into which shells were inserted. The spiral frieze motif can only be reconstructed from the signs we are able to make out on the mortar bedding. A mosaic decoration also must have covered the vault of hall no. 44, but this was later destroyed under Trajan by the construction of a robust central wall which divided the large room into two parallel galleries covered with barrel vaults and closed to the peristyle (no. 20).

Nymphaeum no. 45 seemed to recreate one of the many stage sets that had been popular in wall painting under Nero. Indeed, it was constructed with the intention of creating the illusion of a natural grotto open, originally, to the garden. The water flowed from a waterfall and fed a central basin, while on the ceiling there are fake stalactites (calcareous concretions stuck into the cement of the barrel vault). As in the adjacent rooms, the mosaic of glass-paste tesserae decorated the frieze above the niches and above the waterfall. It was also inserted into the four round medallions (unfortunately taken away in antiquity) placed in the corners in the roof, and into the large central octagon, which is the first example of a figured mosaic carried out on a vault. Polyphemus, with long hair and sturdy muscles, sits on a rock, and receives a goblet of wine from Ulysses. Ulysses is shown in profile, dressed in a short tunic with folds, his pose indicating that he is about to flee. On the ground between the two, there are a few traces of a third figure who might represent one of Ulysses' companions, imprisoned in the cave of the Cyclops. The anatomical details of the bodies and faces of the two characters are stressed in white, while green dominates the muscles, highlighted by gilded tesserae which seem to recall the colour of bronze. According to some scholars, this group may have originated from a sculptural prototype perhaps a product of Rhodes. The theme is related to the sea and nymphs: Polyphemus was born of the union between Neptune, the god of the sea, and the nymph Thoosa, and was in love with the nymph Galatea. Similar groups are known from four other imperial nymphaei: Tiberius' villa in Sperlonga, Claudius' palace in Punta Epitaffio in Baiae, Domitian's villa in Castel Gandolfo and Hadrian's villa in Tivoli. The goblet of wine, by which means Ulysses earns his salvation, gives the scene a dionysiac touch, but the popularity of this theme is also certainly related to the influence of the theatre from the 2nd century BC onwards. In satirical drama, Polyphemus, who has—as in the

Domus Aurea—a long beard and thick hair, comes to be identified with a satyr, a creature which together with nymphs populates the dionysiac world.

The practice of creating a 'natural' space around a display of water is widely attested in the classical age, and was to become more widespread in Renaissance and Baroque villas. The term "nymphaeum" was resurrected to indicate monumental fountains built on sloping ground or inside buildings consisting of porticoes, exhedra, niches and artificial grottoes. It is to the "false grotto" of the 16th century, that Vasari, in the preface of his *Lives*, gave an entire chapter the title *Come di tartari e di colature d'acqua si conducono le fontane rustiche, come nello stucco si murano le telline e le colature delle pietre cotte* ("How water-pipes lead to rustic fountains, how to embed in stucco brick tiles and pipes").

The excavation of the nymphaeum of Ulysses and Polyphemus in the mid1950s brought to light notable marble fragments as well as a fragmentary sculpture of the neo-Attic school (end of 1st century BC) in Greek pentelic marble. The sculpture is the Muse of lyric poetry, Terpsichore, which seems to be an old copy of a Greek model from the Praxiteles school of the 4th century BC.

In room no. 42, substantial alterations were carried out to the initial plan in the final phase of the palace's life. Initially, the

49. Mosaic decoration of the central octagon of the nymphaeum of Ulysses and Polyphemus vault (no. 45)

*50. Statue of the Muse
Terpsichore.
Rome, Domus Aurea*

*51. Room no. 42:
detail of the stucco
decoration with frieze
of figurines surmounted
by relief balusters*

*52. Room no. 42:
detail of the fresco
decoration with a figure
leaning out*

room had an elaborate decoration. On a low marble socle, the fresco was divided into two sections by reliefs in stucco. Slender newels stand out from a frame enclosing an azure-coloured frieze, which is enlivened by a series of slender figurines, some of which are moving, some which are still. Between the newels, the walls open out with fake architectural settings painted in perspective and different characters lean out of them.

There is a fresco under the arch, within a rectangular field which is bordered by a frieze with figures and fantastic animals, a scene peopled with tritons and seahorses which surge out of the waves (marine *thiasos*). At a later date, the room was used differently. A loft was created at the height of the wooden beams which supported a new floor level and a very simple fresco with linear plant elements was painted on the yellow background of the new room.

53. Room no. 42: detail of the intrados: a scene with a marine thiasos

The architectural partition in stucco on a yellow background also appears in the adjacent room no. 41.

The partial visit to the western wing ends within the monumental complex of the nymphaeum of Ulysses and Polyphemus, but the visit to the rooms of the much more architecturally complexed eastern wing begins with two rooms, no. 69 and 70. These have very reduced dimensions and an irregular shape, in which the walls form strange corners and narrow spaces. The anomalies of the plan are due above all to the fact that pre-existent structures belonging to the warehouses (*horrea*) built by the emperor Claudius were incorporated into Nero' palace after the fire of 64 BC, and these influenced the layout. In addition, these rooms (nos. 69 and 70) are the meeting point between the two areas of the palace, east and west, which are different in outline and perhaps also in chronology. An attempt has been made recently to show that

54. Room no. 42: detail of the vault with yellow background: the most recent phase

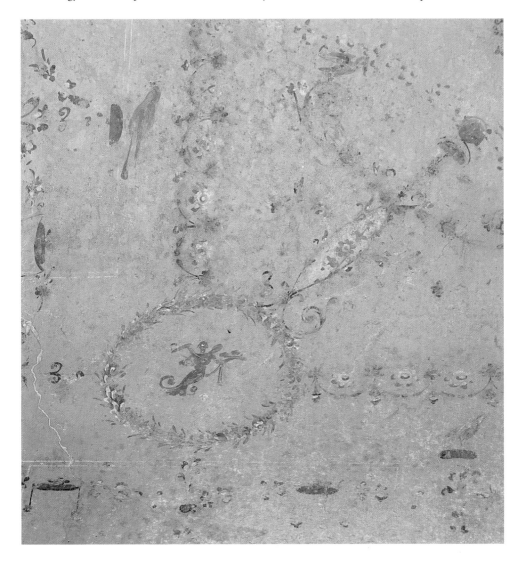

at least nymphaeum no. 45, if not the whole western part, was constructed when rooms no. 69, and perhaps nos. 70 and 46 (not visible), if not indeed the whole eastern sector, were already in existence.

From room no. 69, a portion of the small courtyard no. 51 (the final part of the nymphaeum complex) can be observed through a doorway, now closed off with a glass partition. The room, apsidal at the end, was initially built to bring more light into the adjacent room, no. 45. Indeed, the light was abundant because of the partial semi-cupola covering, and penetrated directly into the nymphaeum through three windows, before these were transformed into niches and faced with marble slabs. The wall decoration decoration of room no. 69 is characterised by the light background and a double order of fake architectural motifs with little perspective: small columns and pavilions are limited to framing the fields where vegetation and small paintings are drawn in simple lines.

Room no. 70 was ruined by water pipes of Trajan's Baths, and preserves only the corners of the frescoed ceiling. The recently restored wall decoration was originally laid above the marble socle, and has architectural façades which lead to a theatrical scene (*frons scaenae*). The painting spreads over two levels: the lower section, which is wider, has a series of perspective openings at the sides of a central passageway, covered by a vault, and framed by yellow pilasters decorated with hanging garlands. The upper, as is seen on the wall at the end, has a sequence of red drapes on which can be seen groups of three small paintings on a dark background with darting figurines in white stucco. To the sides of the central drape, colonnades seem to extend the space beyond the limits of the real wall. Other perspective details, like the painted coffer ceiling to the left of the entrance, give the composition a startling visual effect. From the openings, the aedicules and the transennas, a series of characters seem to lean out towards the interior of the room, also enriched with small paintings including minuscule figures and animals in stucco.

Room 71 once boasted a false ceiling, but today has a restored vault in plastered brick. Originally it had a rather elaborate decoration. In the upper part of the wall, the use of stucco defines the fields, aedicules and pavilions. Lower down, it was probably faced with marble, but later this was replaced by painting on a white background with few ornamental elements. The figurines of wading birds are inserted to be seen inside simple aedicules, alternate with plant candelabra and light floral coronets; in the lower fields there are framed pictures of small birds which have given their name to the room. To the left, beyond the door, we see the slanting wall of Claudius' *horrea*, which has produced a small triangular room (no. 72) with a mosaic floor with small slanted white tesserae. To the right, we see a sequence of rooms (nos. 68, 67, 66 and 65) aligned along one of the sides of the so-called pentagonal courtyard which was erased by Trajan's brick and tufa walls. The waterpipe of Trajan's baths, which cut across the walls of rooms nos. 70 and 71, east-west, enters room no. 74 and eventually crosses, almost at a right angle, another sewer built after room no.

55. The pictorial decoration of
room no. 70 with architectural
perspectives on two levels

56. Detail of the same,
with a character leaning out
and slender stucco figurines

*57. Room no. 71: detail
of the pictorial decoration;
the second phase on the
lower half of the walls with
figurine of wading bird*

73 had been stripped of veneer and buried. Here the panelled painting is divided up by newels painted in a simple manner and framed with a red border decorated with plant motifs. The marbles which faced the lower part of the walls also extended to a complex geometric design on the floor (*opus sectile*) still legible thanks to the imprints on the mortar bed.

In the corridor opposite (no. 74) the decorative scheme is visible above the door; this adds small central aedicules in stucco to the background fresco, in which we note the use of the precious colour purple, extracted from the shells of the Murex species.

Room no. 76, which precedes the grandiose Room of the gilded vault, had a marble veneer, similar to all the rooms next to the main nuclei, which rose very high up the wall. It was only in the last portion, under the false ceiling, that fresco with fake architectural motifs in stucco can be seen.

To the north, room no. 75 still has a threshold in situ, but is closed at the end by the oblique wall of the warehouses of Claudius' age, to which the door belongs, walled in during the Neronian phase when this last passageway was obtained and plastered down to the ground.

The Room of the gilded vault

The heart of the western area was, without doubt, the nymphaeum of Ulysses and Polyphemus and the large hall in front of it. However, while the view from here looked out from the rectangular courtyard, open to the fountain with a play of water at its centre, and accompanied by paintings of gardens along the wall at the end, as far as room no. 15 (opposite no. 44 and similar in terms of size), everything was intimately enclosed within the porticoed area.

In contrast, the perspective from the eastern pavilion opened out towards the south; across the five-sided courtyard, one could pause in the Room of the gilded vault (no. 80), and the eye would descend along the verdant terraces, sloping down to the mirror-like lake, which seemed "like a sea" (Suetonius, *Nero*, 31). The view was cut off by the construction of Trajan's Baths against the front of the monumental triclinium (no. 80), and today this is testimony of the enormous quantity of earth used—before the construction of the baths—to fill in rooms and courtyards.

The room of the gilded vault, on the axis of the five-sided courtyard, was one of the most important rooms of the pavilion. It was enormous, and sumptuous in the marble veneer which rose to cover the whole surface of the walls up to the vault, where pleasant figured frescoes, which are usually attributed to Fabullus, meet the stucco work of the reliefs which gleam with gold-leaf. Today, the ceiling is largely deprived of its decoration, above all at the centre where two large holes reveal the cement which, at the start of recent restoration works, had chunks of a notable size missing. Restoration was thus essential to strengthen the structure. However, the overall composition of the barrel vault remains perfectly legible: elaborate painted stucco cornices frame square, rectangular and round geometric fields which at one time enclosed figured scenes (now completely lost). A further idea of the composition is to be gleaned from a great deal of Renaissance documentation. A watercolour painted in 1538 by Francisco de Hollanda, and preserved in the Escorial Library in Madrid, is a valuable aid for the description of the decorative scheme since it was copied faithfully, except for certain details which imagination altered.

The composition develops within a square in which the effects created by cornices of gilded stucco, together with

58. Room of the gilded vault (no. 80): detail of the vault composition

variations of the colour of the backgrounds, suggest an overall image spread over different levels. As in a tapestry hanging against the sky, a red lozenge-shaped drape seems to open under a circular dome and is held at the corners by four medallions and decorated at the centre with a figured scene inside an inscribed circle in a square. Around the four corner medallions there are rectangular geometric fields containing figured scenes also within squares. The decorative sequence closes with a border formed of two friezes. A continuous row of blue Amazon shields on a red background alternates with azure lozenges, while a series of gilded corbels in relief create an illusory support for the vault decoration.

A comparison with other sources helps us with the interpretation of the figured scenes: data can be obtained from the 16th century drawings still preserved in Madrid or at the Uffizi Gallery in Florence, from a copy dated to the 17th century which is today in the collection at Windsor, and from the 18th century prints by Mirri.

The central medallion, according to the watercolour of Francisco de Hollanda, seems to have illustrated the Rape of Ganymede by Zeus, and to the side, a cupid who is about to fire an arrow at Athena and Hermes.

The copies reveal different subjects on the four corner medallions, each on an azure background (nymph or ephebe astride an animal, ram, bull or horse, at a gallop). The interpretations of the rectangular fields are also contrasted, where more complex scenes would have been expected. It is reasonable to expect images linked to the sea or to the religious sphere, or associated with mythical episodes which were very widespread both in wall painting, particularly in Pompeii, and on reliefs and marble sarcophagi. On the middle axes, on the one hand, we seem to have the illustration of Hippolytus' departure for the hunt, on the other Hephaestus surprising Ares and Venus. Of the remaining eight panels which framed the small medallions on the outside, there are only two known subjects: a satyr playing a flute next to a young woman and Peleus entrusting his small son Achilles to the wisdom of the centaur Chiron.

Innumerable signatures scratched on the surfaces of the frescoed vault witness the flow of visitors which, from the end of the 16th century, let themselves down into the grottoes and walked on the earth which filled the rooms to the level of the vaults. They were able to observe and copy, from close-up, the decorative motifs of the palace, and contributed to the spread of the ornamental repertoire of grotesques. The Gilded Vault in particular, served as a model for many Renaissance ceilings, thanks to the ingenuity of Pinturicchio, Giovanni da Udine and Baldassarre Peruzzi.

Following the rooms on the south side of the five-sided courtyard and crossing room no. 81 (which originally had a false ceiling and marble veneer on the walls), we enter room no. 79. This is a long narrow corridor, with two wings. The first, to the left on entering, is made up of the rear wall of room no. 80 and a parallel wall which hides the irregularity of rooms nos. 77 and 78 (not accessible) caused once more by the presence of the *horrea*. The other wing goes on to connect with the large cryptoporticus no. 92. A large number of signatures are visible on the paintings, not only scratched but also traced in soot. While the first seem attributable to the oldest phases of Renaissance visits, the others can be dated up to the 19th century.

60. Detail of the decoration of the vault of the cryptoporticus no. 79, Mirri 1776

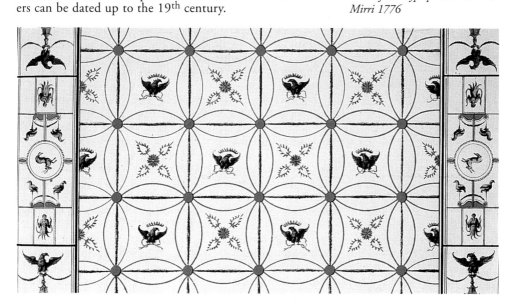

The fresco of the vault has a simple decorative scheme in which, on a clear background, geometric flowers with four petals appear are created by the intersection of red circumferences. These form lozenges which have small paintings inside; in the middle rosettes alternate with eagles with spread wings. The motif has exact parallels with paintings and mosaic floors in Pompeii.

The walls are also without stucco, and are divided into three decorative levels. In the two upper bands, veils hang between delicate architectural elements which frame small landscape paintings and animal figurines.

At the bottom, the decoration becomes more elaborate: theatrical aedicules containing scenic masks surmounted by fantastic animals alternate with rectangular fields with small paintings in the middle, framed by friezes illustrating sphinxes, birds and griffins face-to-face at the sides of a raceme. In a vast area of the walls the design was completely hidden by calcareous formations, but the restoration has meant that we can now fully understand the decorative scheme, and have the possibility to recover other frescoes from the *Domus Aurea*. In particular, on the right hand wall the cleaning of one of the small paintings which is framed by a grotesque frieze has revealed not the landscape repeated frequently in this small fields, but a still-life, an unusual subject for the

61. Cryptoporticus no. 79: overall view of the eastern part

62. Cryptoporticus no. 79: small picture with still-life and frieze with fantastic animals

imperial palace: it is a scene of food, consisting of a ring-shaped loaf of bread on a shelf and the leg of an animal, and underneath something which may be a cut of meat or a fillet of fish.

At the end of corridor no. 79, the first (no. 84) of three consecutive oblique rooms opens. These belonged to Claudius' *horrea* and were incorporated into Nero's palace to join the great eastern cryptoporticus (no. 92), creating small and very irregular connecting areas. As we have already noted the presence of the warehouses in rooms nos. 69 and 70 and along the north side of cryptoporticus no. 79 has indeed led to anomalies and irregularities in the ground plane of the pavilion. These can also bee seen in the rooms which open to the north of corridor no. 62, which also takes advantage of a pre-existing wall.

Room no. 82 is last in a sequence of rooms looking out on to the north side of the courtyard, and is still buried. The following room (no. 83) has a regular rectangular plan, albeit reduced in size because of the presence of older structures. On the walls part of the green and purple background painting remains between balusters in relief stucco. From this room, a passageway which was cut from the wall belonging to Claudius' *horrea* and which has with doorjambs decorated with a small painting supported by volutes, leads to cryptoporticus no. 92.

63-64. Cryptoporticus no. 92: details of the pictorial decoration

Cryptoporticus no. 92

Judging by what is Nero's palace on the Oppian hill, it was designed by the architects, Severus and Celer, to be flooded in light. The widespread application of gold-leaf and the pomp of the precious marbles, along with the help of the sun, must have made the gleaming golden dwelling worthy of an emperor who compared himself to the sun-god *Helios*. As we have said, the main rooms opened on to the south slope, while the opposite side consisted of long corridors, partially buried and obscure, to contain the hillside (nos. 19, 79, 92 and 142). However, in cryptoporticus no. 92, which allowed rapid passage from one courtyard to another through small anterooms nos. 87 and 140, the shadow must have created a suggestive play of chiaroscuro. Indeed, the light entered through the openings high up in the vault supports and passed through the seven splayed windows built lower down in the opposite wall, thus illuminating also the rooms behind.

It is clear that this room of the *Domus Aurea* was visited during the Renaissance, since there are both legible signatures on the ceiling (including that of Giovanni da Udine), and copies of ornamental motifs, whose loudest echo is to be heard in the school of Raphael. In the *Loggetta* of Cardinal Bibbiena's apartment in the Vatican, Giovanni da Udine was inspired precisely by the division of the vault with central carpet decoration, the architectural motifs on the supports and the white background crowded with grotesques.

The walls of cryptoporticus no. 92 have a decoration which is generally identified as the simplest type, consisting of fres-

coes on all the surfaces with a light background, on which
the fantastic repertoire repeats itself with an endless series of
variants. But the plant and animal elements, enclosed in
square or rectangular panels, which figure also at the centre
of the splayed windows, are joined by subjects taken from
the Egyptian world, such as the god with the dog's head,
Anubis, seen in the vertical frieze at the end of the right
hand wall.

Two stucco mouldings highlight the line of the vault. High-
er up, on both sides of the central motif of the ceiling, there
is a wide yellow band with delicate aedicules decorated with
small animals, alternating with arabesques and racemes, and
crowded with dolphins and griffins. This creates an image of
tapestries hanging one over another for the whole length of
the ceiling. A variety of frieze types (with acanthus spirals,
flower corollas, palmettes, sphinxes, griffins, vases and lyres)
subdivide each of the rectangular panels within each carpet

65. Loggetta of cardinal Bibbiena,
detail of the wall with frescoes
by Giovanni da Udine
Rome, Vatican Palaces

design. Correspondingly, there is a multitude of depictions of birds, swans, panthers, lions and legendary animals between stalks and garlands interwoven in a checked pattern, woven in straight lines or diagonals. In the same style, rendered with rapid brushstrokes, figures are traced which animate the white background of the fresco divided by light floral stalks on the arch which crosses the corridor. This arch hides a water pipe which goes from the upper floor down to feed nymphaeum no. 124, which is inserted into the complex of the octagonal room. Above the arch, the next rectangular panel at the centre of the vault appears to be decorated differently to previous panels. Four friezes, with the usual repertoire of plant and animal elements, are superimposed so as to suggest a sequence of carpets, arranged one above the other. The checked weaving is then taken up and repeated in the rectangular panels which adorn the rest of the ceiling.

Cryptoporticus no. 92 runs in a straight line for about 70 metres joining the end of another corridor (no. 142) which is still buried up to the level of the vault but symmetrical in layout to no. 79. In the first wing the vault, bordered at the bottom by a relief cornice, has a decorated border with birds at the sides or vegetation or lyres which alternate with running animals. In the second wing the border is made up of

66. Cryptoporticus no. 92: detail of the decoration of a splayed window

ribbons interwoven with red flowers or fantastic animals facing floral goblets. Over the whole surface of the vault elegant
vine stalks with multi-coloured flowers create a sequence of
rhombs and circles with spread-winged eagles or panthers.
On the opposite side of corridor no. 92 a series of passages
(nos. 112, 113, 114, 115 and 131), currently closed to the
public, connected the north of the palace to the front open
on to the valley.
The walls of room no. 114 (the Room of masks) are divided
by friezes in rectangular panels, within which small landscape pictures are inserted; they open at the centre through
painted architectural motifs from which garlands hang. The
upper part of the decorative sequence consists of a series of
very airy and complex architectural elements which open the
space out into a number of perspective planes.
The painted façade is enriched with multiple decorative mo-

*67. Cryptoporticus no. 92,
room no. 86: detail of the
pictorial decoration
with slender architectures
on a white background*

*68. Cryptoporticus
no. 92: detail of the
frieze with the
representation of Anubis;
at the side one of the
perspective aedicules*

*69. Cryptoporticus
no. 92: detail of the
decoration of the archlet*

tifs including the theatrical masks which give the room its name. Room no. 131 was endowed originally with a false ceiling bordered by a white stucco cornice, and has two levels of complex architectural motifs painted with a great visual awareness. The succession of perspectives is highlighted by light blue spiral balusters in the background, and the presence of characters who are arranged in front of the monumental façade or inside every single illusory pavilion. The representation is bordered at the top by a frieze with stucco figurines on a red and blue background.

In the rooms 85 and 86 there are a number of doors which have been blocked in (no. 85) or cut (no. 86) to a relatively low height since the floor level of the *horrea* to which they belonged must have been much lower. It is on these pre-existing walls in brick, which have no veneer, that there are architectural elements in travertine on the sides of the lintels and broken brackets which must have supported the loft of the upper floor. Since they were passages, they had a very simple fresco design. In room no. 86, on the light background laid on the walls, the usual small landscape pictures are found articulated in three bands by linear divisions which only hint at architectural perspectives. In the upper band a motif is added which consists of two suspended vases in the form of floral goblets, decorated perhaps with fabric or ribbons. Although the style therefore is rather poor and of a minor tone, a strange detail in room no. 85 represents a note of vivacity: a fake window opens on an illusory lake landscape, enlivened by different figurines.

Backtracking, the route of the visit continues into the small room no. 87. A pavilion can be seen above the lintel of the door, enclosed at the top by a white stucco cornice, with two projecting bodies at the sides which open onto a another

70. Cryptoporticus no. 92: detail of the vault with the carpet decoration in the watercolour by F. Weege (1913)

*71. Cryptoporticus no. 92:
detail of the vault
with the carpet decoration*

background with architectural perspective. There is a lively use of the most precious colours, among which purple, azure and cinnabar red stand out.

The next room (no. 88) appears to be completely lacking in decoration; however, the partial removal and organisation of the earth used to fill in the building by Trajan outside the room has restored to view part of the palace façade. Near the courtyard it was decorated there is a painting high on the wall of buildings in notable perspective.

The next room (no. 89) can probably be identified as a library on the basis of the niches and apses which were dug out of the walls and originally faced with marble slabs. Actually there is no trace within these niches of shelves for books, and neither does the position of the room seem suitable for this use: according to Vitruvius, papyrus rolls should not be preserved in rooms facing south since an excessive amount of light and heat make them fade. It is possible that the niches were intended for display of reliefs and statues, as in the nymphaeum of Ulysses and Polyphemus. Few traces remain of paintings on the upper part of the walls and on the basin of the apse. This was decorated with a fake awning, a motif which was to be taken up again in the Renaissance.

In room no. 90, as in rooms nos. 88 and 89, the entrance door to the courtyard was blocked by one of Trajan's walls. The room opens on the opposite side towards rooms nos. 94 and 95. In the white background of the painting in the first

72. Cryptoporticus no. 142: detail of the vault with frieze: ribbons and flowers

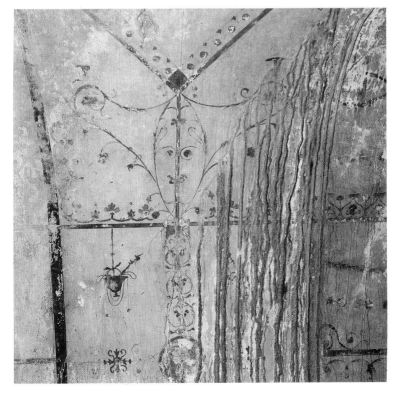

73. Cryptoporticus no. 142: detail of the vault with floral stalks

room, linear divisions are repeated over a number of levels, and floral stalks descend from them to frame single figures of small fantastic animals, centaurs and birds. Above a door a character leans out from a balcony, leaning on a transenna. The short triangular cubicle no. 91, in which a small piece of the false ceiling frescoed in violet is preserved, joins corridor no. 96 and from here, turning right, we leave the palace and enter the five-sided courtyard. The large brick wall and its extension support a barrel vault creating, in Trajan's age, a closed gallery where Nero's structure had been an open space. High up, partially incorporated into the cement of Trajan's vault, two travertine corbels perhaps supported originally the short wooden cover of the façade. Here in the upper part, the decoration consists of an elaborate stucco cornice. This borders a frieze in which aedicules are enlivened by figures in relief which alternate with square frescoes; in the single example still legible, a theatre wing, drawn between the light blue of the sky and the green of the gardens, may represent the courtyard of the *Domus Aurea*, where it opens towards the valley.

The surface of the walls in the Neronian phase appear to be covered with the cement bed for marble veneer slabs, while the large door of room no. 116 was blocked off during the Trajanic construction by an unplastered wall. We re-enter the interior of the pavilion through the door of corridor no. 117, above which on the inside is a painting with a sacred subject representing three characters around a image of Minerva. From here we enter room no. 116 which preserves its mosa-

*74. Room of masks
(no. 114): overall view
of the painted decoration*

*75. Giovanni da Udine
(1487-1564), decoration of the
calotte of an apse with false
grotesque decorated awning.
Rome, Villa Madama*

76. Room no. 131: detail of the frieze with stucco figurines on the impost line of the vault

77. Room no. 85: false window open on a fantastic landscape

78. Room no. 86:
detail of the painted decoration

ic floor with black and white tesserae arranged to form a geometric pattern of squares and triangles arranged around hexagons. On the walls, which have no stucco, the fresco is laid in large areas with a black background above a red socle. A low marble socle and a lowered ceiling characterise corridor no. 117 and its extension (nos. 120 and 121), which we have to imagine open to the valley.

The Room of Achilles at Scyros
The marble slabs rose up to cover well over half of the walls in the Room of Achilles at Scyros (no. 119), where the combination of architectural decoration sequence in stucco and painted perspectives enlivened by figures, are articulated

with rigour and grandeur, making it one of the greatest examples of painting of the so-called "fourth style". Discovered in the 20th century, it is one of the few main halls which do not make up part of the Renaissance route.

Stucco is predominant: it frames the fields on the barrel vault and throws into relief the apse with the two half-column shafts decorated with small pictures of fantastic figurines inserted into the scale-like design—this in fact is a reprisal of the taste for polychrome marbles, used in great quantity in Nero's palace. On the walls, stucco pilasters with composite capitals divide up the architectural motifs which are painted with realistic perspectives, and it enriches the white background and the colours of the painting with the addition of gold-leaf. The painting is enriched with details and a meticulous style: the pilasters become plant stalks, and inside the shell-like basin there are vine tendrils full of birds, winged busts, lyres, at the side of which minuscule animals are arranged symmetrically. Once more the stucco adorns the backgrounds with friezes and garlands and it is possible that the scene at the centre of the ceiling reveal who the artist was—Fabullus, mentioned in the ancient sources.

The *Achilles at Scyros* panel, which gives its name to the room, refers to the Homeric tale: Thetis, attempting to save her son Achilles from death in war, sends him to Scyros, a small island near Euboea. King Lycomedes hides Achilles—dressed as a woman—among his daughters. The scene shows Achilles amongst the girls; from the gifts brought by the shrewd Ulysses (the helmeted figure with a high crest), Achilles chooses the weapons and thus betrays his identity; he then leaves his female clothes aside, ready to go to battle. By means of a rather complex composite syntax, the artist has wisely chosen to paint one of the characters in the foreground with his back to us, providing the scene with a particular vivacity.

At the corners of the central panel, four smaller pictures are arranged with plant motifs, and on the axes other panels, one of which shows a draped female figure holding an amphora. In the southern part of the vault there is a dionysiac scene: four characters, vine leaves on their heads, are reclining next to a flute player. The whole central motif is enclosed within a Greek fret frieze. All around, a second frieze with painted scenes, portrays reclining characters associated with the dionysiac world; one of these has a goblet in his hand (*kantharos*), another a cornucopia or a chest of grapes. The sequence of the scene is interrupted on every side at the centre, by a stucco figurine on a red background stands out, of which only the outline remains.

Among the small pictures, the remaining counterpoised 'T' shaped spaces are enriched by winged female busts emerging from floral corollas and generating vine stalks and racemes. The vault decoration continues on the lenght-wise with two bands, each subdivided into three panels; all that remains is the central panel in the right hand wall with traces of a painted character in movement, and the floral cornices of the individual fields, animated by sphinxes or winged female

81-84: Room of Achilles at Scyros (no. 113): details of the pictorial wall decoration

figures, arranged symmetrically at the sides of the goblets. An elaborate polychrome cornice in stucco borders the vault. Underneath, on the walls, including the apse, complex architectural motifs in perspective are seen, with monochrome background characters or small pictures, where stucco figurines were inserted. The perspectives of the last band at the top are occupied by fantastic animals, heraldically arranged at the sides of the central motifs, and by winged female figures crouching and supporting small pictures.

The Octagonal Room complex

Continuing along corridor no. 121, we arrive at the octagonal room complex, the focus point of the whole pavilion on the Oppian hill, created in the heart of the city, looking out on woods, gardens and water displays in imitation of maritime villas.

The eastern wing is inserted between the valley constructions which were set out on the terraced hill; the layout had already been sensed by De Romanis in the 19th century, and was clarified after the explorations in the seventies carried out in the upper level by the Rome Soprintendenza Archeologica.

The building has two identical wings facing each other, which are inserted into the complex of the octagon (originally—and mistakenly—thought to be the culmination of the architectural sequence). It had a great influence on Roman architecture since it was the first monument in Rome which exploited the new, awareness of the possibilities offered by the use of concrete in vaults to create a revolutionary architectural vision of internal space: an octagonal room inserted into a palace divided traditionally into rooms with a rectangular plan. Still today, even without the original scenic landscape, the octagonal room and the circle of rooms surrounding it encourage the visitor to stop and contemplate the particular effects of light and colour obtained by means of articulated architectural forms. At the centre, a space which is completely free generates an octagonal structure on which a vault rests, forming a pavilion with eight corners; near the central aperture, it takes on the appearance of a cupola with a hemispherical surface. The abundant light entering the room through the wide oculus in the concrete of the vault reaches the five radial rooms by means of an ingenious system of windows splayed towards the bottom, positioned between the walls of the octagon and the extrados of the cupola, which appears in each of the rooms. The sense of delicateness which the daring architectural solution manages to achieve is highlighted by the fact that the vault seems to be supported only by the corners; these are formed by the wide architraves of the passages into the surrounding rooms, in actual fact discharging the load on to their radial walls, too. By looking at the overall plan we see that while the octagon adheres to the front of the building, the two rooms nos. 122 and 126, which are characterised by large rectilinear niches, are inserted only indirectly into the façade, through corridors nos. 121 and 127. Room no. 124 opens

85. View of the octagonal room (no. 128)

along the main axis and is in fact a nymphaeum. Beyond the apse of the rear wall, there was a waterfall—we can see the remains of the mortar bed with traces of two channels—fed by the water from the upper floor through the arch of cryptoporticus no. 92 and adorned perhaps by the presence of a statue, as a base still in situ would seem to indicate. To the sides of the nymphaeum, rooms nos. 123 and 125 follow a crossed plan; the three wings have large niches with barrel vaults on three levels. The fourth wing acts as passage to the octagon and this also has a barrel vault. The rectangular area at the centre, produced by the cross-over of the four sides, develops a cross vault, one of the two oldest examples from Roman architecture.

Marble veneer adorned the walls of every room in the complex. However, the decorative sequences on the vaults seem to differentiate the functions of the different rooms. The ceiling of the barrel vault of room no. 124 had a mosaic decoration related to the presence of water; but it is no longer possible to describe its composition, although it was framed with a shell motif inserted into a red band, and bordered by two rows of white tesserae, just as in the nymphaeum of Ulysses and Polyphemus of the western wing. The six small triangular rooms which connect the circle of rooms and create an ambulatory around the octagon are characterised by false ceilings bordered by stucco cornices, which have unfortunately collapsed. On the short walls the fresco has been partially preserved: delicate garlands and linear divisions, in live-

ly colours, divide the fields surmounted by dolphins or winged sphinxes, in which cupids and other figurines appear. Rooms nos. 122 and 126 also have barrel vaults and, even though there are few traces, they were probably adorned with stuccoes. In the rooms with cross-shaped plans the vaults of the wing which connected with the central room are decorated with lozenges in relief and medallions framing a small picture, while in the other three wings the niches on the lower floor have bands painted in red and bordered by stucco cornices—to emphasis the diagonals of the vault— and a central medallion. Inside the segments, small pictures with a purple background contained figured scenes. The niches of the upper floor seem to be without decoration. We might suppose that there were covers made from canvass or tapestry and interpret these inaccessible rooms as exhibition spaces used for statues.

Even in the octagonal room, there was never a fixed facing to hide the rough surface of the vault, which still has the imprints of the planks used to contain the concrete as it was laid. Apart from an unlikely interpretation that redates the building to the Flavian age and considers the eastern wing unfinished in Nero's times, the absence of decoration has obviously led to the conclusion that the furnishing had been temporary, and had been fabric or wood. In both cases, two concentric grooves around the oculus, in the mortar of the vault extrados, which are no longer visible, may indicate where a supporting frame was inserted. The function of the room with the light oculus, lends itself to different interpretations; particularly suggestive is the identification of the octagonal room with the main dining room, described by Suetonius, which rotated continuously, day and night, like the world (Suetonius, *Nero*, 31). If this were the case, we need to imagine not only that the vault was covered by a calotte in perishable material, but that

86. The octagonal room: partial view of the ambulatory

87. View of the octagonal room no. 122, with splayed window open on the extrados of the vault

88. Octagonal room complex: detail of the pictorial decoration of one of the six triangular connecting rooms

---

this in some way could also rotate. There is no actual archaeological evidence for this interpretation, and no trace has been found of any hydraulic mechanism which could create motion activated by the water coming from the cascade. This water fell into the main basin, disappearing under the floor, aligned with nymphaeum no. 124.

Another hypothesis for the octagonal room is that it was purely decorative, i.e. that it was an empty space for contemplation, where guests could recline languidly on the triclinium beds of the four radial rooms. This theory can be expanded through an analysis of the testimony of Pliny: the room could be one of the halls of the Golden House intended for luxurious furnishings (*sellaria*: Pliny, *Natural History*, XXXIV, 84). Indeed, like the upper niches of rooms nos. 123 and 125, the octagonal room is to be interpreted as an exhibition space. The grandiose internal space with its new architectural forms was the ideal place in which works of art, illuminated by the light from the central oculus of the vault, can be perfectly admired from all angles by people who can walk around them thanks to the octagonal plan.

The Room of Hector and Andromache

The last room in the visit, at the end of the excavated area of the pavilion, is the Room of Hector and Andromache (no. 129) which, in respect to the octagon, is symmetrically to the Room of Achilles in Scyros and repeats the same decorative scheme based on the union of painting and stucco. The room is divided geometrically with a rectangle inserted

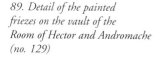

89. Detail of the painted friezes on the vault of the Room of Hector and Andromache (no. 129)

90. Graphic reconstruction of the same painted friezes

first frieze

second frieze

third frieze

side band

91. Room of Hector and Andromache (no. 129): the painting with the scene of the parting of Hector and Andromache

92. Room of Hector and Andromache (no. 129): detail of the decoration of the side band with female figurine and small picture with stucco figurines

into the centre of the vault with smaller pictures in its corners; one of them preserves the design of an octagon with corners terminating in floral goblets around a stucco figurine, which is now lost. Aligned with the axes, another four panels must have been decorated with painted figured scenes. Two of them represent satyrs and maenads dancing. The central panel is framed by three friezes and separated by stucco cornices. The first has a simple Greek fret motif; the second, which is larger, has five small pictures at the centre of every side which are transformed in the corners into an 'L' shaped geometric figure. In each of these a plant stalk forms a lozenge as a background for a relief figure. The intermediate spaces which take on the form of counterpoised 'Ts' are decorated with griffins facing each other at the sides of a floral goblet. The third frieze encloses the vault: it consists of vegetation between two winged figurines emerging from acanthus spirals on which two cats are arranged symmetrically, and alternates with a small picture with a monochrome background for figurines, now lost. On the long sides of the room, the vault extends in two wide bands, each enriched with a central panel with a painted figured scene and two rectangular panels at the sides which are bordered by elegant stalks. Small coloured rectangles, alternating with gilded stucco corbels around the panels contribute to an effect of depth. Inside the only rectangular panel preserved, a slender painted female figurine is inserted between two small pictures with a dark background which have the silhouette of small high-relief characters (this panel has been removed).

In the painting in the centre of the vault the theme is linked to the mythical world of the sea. A cupid holding a casket in his hands accompanies the main part of the painting, of which only the figure of a Triton remains, robust, muscular, rowing and looking backwards towards another character,

93. Room of Hector and Andromache (no. 129): geometric composition of the vault decoration

who is only partially preserved. The painting was identified as the wedding of Amphitrite in two drawings by Francesco Bartoli, now at the Uffizi, dated 16th century; this identification would seem to be confirmed also by the presence, among the waves, of a dolphin, ridden by another cupid which, according to legend (Apollodorus, III, 13, 5) must have had a primary role in the event. Indeed, with great passion he championed the cause of the sea god and persuaded the Nereid to marry Neptune, who in gratitude, immortalised his image among the stars. According to another interpretation the painting portrays the mother of Achilles, Thetis, ploughing the waves on the chariot, flanked by tritons.

The painting in the centre of the left-hand band has an armed virile figure, turned towards a woman with a baby in her arms and, alongside, another female figure with her right hand extended, supporting an object. In the background, we see the walls of a city and a smaller figure under an arch seen in perspective. The subject is taken from the Homeric tale; Hector, before meeting Achilles in mortal combat, salutes his wife Andromache and his little son Astyanax on the walls of Troy at the Scaea gate.

The different interpretation identifies the male figure as the Roman hero Coriolanus meeting his mother and his spouse; but this reading, relating to an episode of Roman history is unusual and contrary to the whole decorative scheme of the palace, which promoted the philhellenic culture of the emperor, seems to have no basis.

On the opposite side, the symmetrical scene represents a female figure with a diadem in her hair; she faces another female figure and advances with her arm outstretched towards a man but she is kept from going forward by a cupid pulling her dress. In the background behind the man—perhaps here the walls of a city—another male character appears. The meeting is commonly associated with the love, encouraged by Aphrodite and Cupid, between the young Paris and Helen. Helen is represented with a crown as the wife of the Spartan king Menelaus, who, for the ignominy suffered, then convinced the Greeks to declare war on the Trojans. However, the theme could also be the myth of the Greek hero Protesilaus, who was killed by Hector but who was given the chance by Zeus to return from the reign of the dead to meet his wife Laodamia once more. If this second hypothesis is accepted, the male character in the background represents the god charged with guiding souls in the afterlife (*Hermes Psykhopompos*) and both the episodes represent conjugal love. The choice of the passages, taken from the Iliad, favour the tales in which the heroes are seen at their most human and sorrowful, rather than being exhalted for their warlike valour. An elaborate polychrome cornice runs along all the sides, framing the wall decoration. To the south, painted perspectives enriched with architectural elements in stucco, frame other figures. Only a few decorative elements and the ribbing of the apse made of shells remain, which could not have been very different from those preserved in the basin of the twin room (no. 119).

The minuscule ornamental details, the stucco marks and the relief figurines reserved for the top of the walls and ceiling, were drawn meticulously, and took no notice of the dimensions of the room; therefore they cannot be appreciated from below.

The Homeric poem is, it seems, the main source of inspiration for the decoration in the rooms of the *Domus Aurea*, and accords with the ancient tradition in which Nero, accompanied by the lyre, sang of the fall of Troy while Rome burned in the summer of AD 64. In this sense, the episodes represented might include a reference to the ideologies in fashion during Nero's principate and symbolise the desire of the emperor to lead Rome, resurrected from the ashes, to the new golden age. The link between the two cities assumes a particular significance now that archaeological discoveries in ancient Lavinium have largely confirmed the tradition that Aeneas landed on the coasts of Latium: he was the Trojan hero who escaped from the destruction of the city, with his little son Iulus from whom the noble Julio-Claudians boasted descendance: "Now fix your gaze, observe your Roman people / Caesar is he, with the entire lineage of Julius, / who will come under the vast splendour of the heavens" (Virgil, *Aeneid*, VI, 788-790).

94. Room of Hector and Andromache (no. 129): detail of the decoration of the vault with satyrs and maenads dancing

THE EXCAVATIONS IN THE PAVILION ON THE OPPIAN HILL

16th century

The first excavations inside the pavilion on the Oppian hill had a clearly antiquarian character. The clearance of earth was non-systematic, mostly so that the pictorial decorations could be copied and drawings and engravings made from them.

17-18th century

The mid-17th and early years of the 18th centuries: exploration of certain rooms by Pier Sante Bartoli. A book of drawings was the result: P.S. Bartoli, G.P. Bellori, *Le pitture antiche delle grotte di Roma e del sepolcro de Nasoni*, Rome 1706.
1758-1769: under pope Clement XIII the first regular excavations were carried out, entrusted to the English architect Cameron, published in: C. Cameron, *The Baths of the Romans*, London 1772.
1774: the Roman antiquarian Mirri had sixteen rooms cleared: from the drawings of decorations copied by the painters Smugliewicz and Brenna, an album of sixty engravings was obtained which were sold on the antiquarian market: L. Mirri, G. Carletti, *Le antiche camere delle Terme di Tito e le loro pitture*, Rome 1776.

19th century

Regular excavations began, with a renewed interest in Roman antiquity, during the papacy of Pius VII.
1811-1814: excavations of A. De Romanis, during which fifty rooms were explored and partially cleared of earth infills. The work and the new plan of the pavilion were edited in: A. De Romanis, *Le antiche camere esquiline dette comunemente delle Terme di Tito*, Rome, 1882.

20th century

Work and explorations inside the pavilion were renewed after almost a century.
1912-1914: new excavations under the direction of Prof. A. Muñoz, director of the Regia Soprintenza ai Monumenti del Lazio e degli Abruzzi.
In the same years F. Weege edited *Das goldene Haus des Nero* in JdI, 28, 1913, p. 127-244.
1935-1936: the Archaeological Park of the Colle Oppio is created, the work of Antonio Muñoz, in which the ruins of Trajan's Baths are given new streets and gardens, inspired by Piranesi. The existence of Nero's palace was completely forgotten: A. Muñoz, *Il parco di Traiano*, Rome 1936.
1939; new works inside the *Domus Aurea* directed by the Soprintendenza ai Monumenti del Lazio, under Prof. Alberto Terenzio, of which there is news in: A. Terenzio, BCom, 1938, p. 244 f.
After the pause due to the war, new excavations, together with consolidation work, were carried out by the Soprintendenza ai Monumenti del Lazio.
1954-1957: the Soprintendenza, directed by Prof. Carlo Ceschi, with the organisation of the work entrusted to architect Sanguinetti, cleared earth from unexplored rooms. The first results were published in: Sanguinetti, *Lavori recenti nella Domus Aurea*, "Palladio", 7, 1957, p. 126 f.
From 1969: the Soprintendenza Archeologica di Roma began an excavations and a waterproofing programme for the vaults which loowed, among other things, the exploration of the upper floor, which had never been investigated, under the direction of Dr. Laura Fabbrini. The results are edited in: L. Fabbrini, *Il piano superiore del quartiere orientale*, MemPontAc, 15, 1982, p. 5 f.

BIBLIOGRAPHY

Bibliography concerning the excavations and first explorations of the *Domus Aurea* is included in the chronological summary of excavations. The criteria chosen for the journals are those of the Archäologische Bibliographie.

N. Ponce, *Description des bains de Titus*, Paris 1786.

G. Giovannoni, *La cupola della Domus Aurea neroniana*, in "Atti del I Congresso nazionale di storia dell'architettura" (19-31 October 1936), Florence 1938, p. 3 f.

H.P. L'Orange, *Domus Aurea, der Sonnenpalast*, SymbOslo, suppl. 11, 1942, p. 68 f.

C.C. Van Essen, *La topographie de la Domus Aurea Neronis*, "Mededelingen der Koninklijke Nederlandse Akademie von Wetenschappen: Afd. Letterkunde", 17,12, 1954, p. 371-398.

J.B. Ward-Perkins, *Nero's Golden House*, "Antiquity", 30, 1956, p. 209-219.

F. Sanguinetti, *Il mosaico del Ninfeo ed altre recenti scoperte nella Domus Aurea*, BArchit, 12, 1958, p. 35-45.

G. Zander, *La Domus Aurea: nuovi problemi architettonici*, BArchit, 12, 1958, p. 47-64.

A. Boëthius, *The Golden House of Nero*, Michigan 1960.

G. Zander, *Nuovi studi e ricerche sulla Domus Aurea*, "Palladio", 15, 1965, p. 157-159.

N. Dacos, *Per la storia delle Grottesche. La riscoperta della Domus Aurea*, BdA, 51, 1966, p. 43-49.

N. Dacos, *Fabullus et l'autre peintre de la Domus Aurea*, DialA, 2, 1968, p. 210-226.

N. Dacos, *La découverte de la Domus Aurea et la formation des Grotesques à la Renaissance*, London-Leiden 1969.

H. Lavagne, *Le nymphée au Polyphème de la Domus Aurea*, MEFRA, 82, 1970, p. 673-721.

H. Prückner, S. Storz, *Beobachtungen im Oktogon der Domus Aurea*, RM, 81, 1974, p. 323-339.

P.G. Warden, *The Domus Aurea Reconsidered*, "Journal of the Society of Architectural Historians", 40, 1981, p. 271-278.

Y. Perrin, *Nicolas Ponce et la Domus Aurea de Neron: une documentation inédite*, MEFRA, 94, 1982, p. 833-891.

W.J. Peters, P.G.P. Meyboom, *The Roots of Provincial Roman Painting: Results of Current Research in Nero's Domus Aurea*, in *Roman Provincial Wall: Painting of the Western Empire*, Oxford 1982, p. 33-74.

L. Fabbrini, *Domus Aurea: una nuova lettura planimetrica del palazzo sul colle Oppio*, AnalRom, Suppl. X, 1983, p. 169-186.

P.G.P. Meyboom, *Fabullus démasqué*, in *Om de tuin geleid. Feestbundel Prof. W.J.T. Peters*, Nijmegen 1984, p. 31-39.

L. Fabbrini, *I corpi edilizi che condizionarono la realizzazione del progetto del palazzo esquilino di Nerone*, RendPontAc, 58, 1985-1986, p. 129-179.

F.L. Ball, *The Masonry Chronology of Nero's Domus Aurea*, Diss. University of Virginia, 1987.

G. Rocco, *Alcune osservazioni sul valore architettonico dell'antica decorazione parietale: la Domus Aurea di Nerone*, "Palladio", 1, 1988, pp. 121-134.

D. Hemsoll, *Reconstructing the Octagonal Dining Room of Nero's Golden House*, "Architectural History", 32, 1988, p. 1-17.

D. Hemsoll, *The Architecture of Nero's Golden House*, in *Architecture and Architectural Sculpture in the Roman Empire*, edited by M. Henig, Oxford 1990, p. 10-38.

G. Arciprete, *Domus Aurea: una statua di musa dall'Antiquarium*, BA, 9, 1991, p. 67-72, 76-77.

P.G.P. Meyboom, E. Moormann, *Domus Aurea: appunti sul padiglione della Domus Aurea neroniana sul colle Oppio*, BA, 16-18, 1992, p. 139-145.

W.J.T. Peters, P.G.P. Meyboom, *Decorazione ed ambiente nella Domus Aurea di Nerone*, in *Functional and spatial analysis of wall painting*, Proceedings of the Fifth International Congress on Ancient Wall Painting (Amsterdam, 8-12 September 1992), Leiden 1993, p. 59-63.

F.L. Ball, *A Reappraisal of Nero's Domus Aurea*, JRA, Suppl. 11, Ann Arbor 1994, p. 183-254.

C. Krause, *Domus Tiberiana, I. Gli scavi*, BA, 25-27, 1994.

Lexicon Topographicum Urbis Romae, edited by E.M. Steinby, I, Rome 1993, see *Colossus: Nero* (C. Lega); II, Rome 1995, see *Domus Aurea* (A. Cassatella); *Domus Aurea: vestibulum* (A. Cassatella, S. Panella); *Domus Aurea: area dello stagnum* (C. Panella); *Domus Aurea: porticus triplices miliariae* (E. Papi); *Domus Aurea: il palazzo sull'Esquilino* (L. Fabbrini); *Domus Aurea: complesso del Palatino* (A. Cassatella); *Domus Transitoria* (M. de Vos).

M. Medri, *SUET. Nero, 31. 1. Elementi e proposte per la ricostruzione della Domus Aurea*, in *Meta Sudans, 1. Un'area sacra "in Palatio" e la valle del Colosseo prima e dopo Nerone*, Rome 1996, p. 165-180.

E.M. Moormann, "*Vivere come un uomo*": l'uso dello spazio nella Domus Aurea, in *Horti Romani*, Proceedings of the International Congress (Rome, 4-6 May 1995), edited by M. Cima, E. La Rocca, Rome 1998, p. 345-361.

E. Champlin, *God and Man in the Golden House*, in *Horti Romani*, see above, p. 333-344.

Domus Aurea: la decorazione pittorica del palazzo neroniano nell'album delle "Terme di Tito" conservato al Louvre, text by M. N. Pinot de Villechenon, Milan 1998.

PHOTOGRAPHS AND PLANS

Photographs, if not otherwise
indicated, are by Eugenio Monti
(Soprintendenza Archeologica di
Roma) together with the Studio
Cozzi - Scribani.

The overall plan of the pavilion
on the Oppian hill has been
realized by the Studio di
Architettura of Giovanni
Longobardi and Andrea Mandara
for the Soprintendenza
Archeologica di Roma.

1: from *La fascination de l'antique
1700-1770. Rome découverte,
Rome inventée,* Catalogue of the
Exhibition (Lyon, Musée de la
civilisation gallo-romaine,
20 December - 14 March 1999),
Azzano San Paolo 1998.

4: from Medri 1996
(see bibliography).

5: from *Roma Antiqua. "Envòis"
degli architetti francesi (1788-
1924). L'area archeologica centrale,*
Rome 1985.

6: reconstruction and drawing
by Elio Paparatti (Soprintendenza
Archeologica di Roma).

7, 8: Luciano Pedicini - Archivio
dell'Arte.

22, 23, 25, 47, 60: from *Domus
Aurea* 1998 (see bibliography).

34, 35: Musei Capitolini Archives
by Lorenzo De Masi).

36: Scala Archives.

48: reconstruction and drawing
by Elio Paparatti (Soprintendenza
Archeologica di Roma).

This book was printed for Mondadori Electa S.p.A.
at Tipografia La Piramide (Rome) in the year 2003